FROM ASAHI TO ZEBRAS

To Keith Olbermann,
with respect and gratitude
for being a voice of intelligence
and reason.

8/27/2018

Ralph Pearce

P.S. Feel free to peruse or toss
into the recycling bin! Chapter 4, the
San Jose Asahi play a dramatic game against the
Tokyo Giants!

FROM ASAHI TO ZEBRAS

JAPANESE AMERICAN BASEBALL IN SAN JOSE, CALIFORNIA

RALPH M. PEARCE

Foreword by Stephen Fugita

JAPANESE AMERICAN MUSEUM OF SAN JOSE

ISBN No. 0-9742157-1-6

Front Cover Photograph: Courtesy of Tetsuko Zaima
Back Cover Photograph: Gabriel Ibarra
Cover Design: Cathleen Fortune, Fortune^2 Design
Interior Design: Bonnie Montgomery and Cathleen Fortune
Editing and Production: Bonnie Montgomery, Bay & Valley Publishers
Printing and Binding: BR Printers, San Jose, California

The author gratefully acknowledges a generous grant from the Sourisseau Academy, Department of History, San Jose State University.

Published by the
Japanese American Museum of San Jose (JAMsj)
535 North Fifth Street
San Jose, California 95112
(408) 294-3138; Fax (408) 294-6157
www.jamsj.org

FIRST EDITION

Printed in the United States of America

To my mother
Joyce Meredith Pearce
for a lifetime of love, encouragement and inspiration

and

to all the players and fans who simply loved the game

CONTENTS

FOREWORD

As a child growing up in the Midwest, I remember my father and his Nisei buddies animatedly discussing their exploits playing baseball on Japanese American teams in California. At the time, I did not fully appreciate the significance of the sport in their lives or in that of the Japanese American community. Only many years later did I begin to fathom how important this seemingly quintessential American pastime was to the players, their families, and the ethnic community. It built strong bonds among team members and between widely dispersed Nikkei communities across the state of California.

Before World War II, supporting and watching baseball was one of the main recreational outlets for the Issei who otherwise seemingly worked endlessly on their farms or in their small businesses. For the Nisei, it was not only a social and recreational outlet among themselves, but it also provided positive contact with members of the larger society during an era characterized by widespread discrimination against Japanese Americans. Even after Pearl Harbor, when the community was locked up behind barbed wire, baseball was a popular pastime which helped many weather the stresses of the period.

Several years ago, I had the pleasure of meeting Ralph Pearce and was awed by his passion for Nikkei baseball. In fact, I was so impressed that I tagged along on several of his interviews of former San Jose Asahi and Zebra players to learn more. In subsequent years, Ralph has continued to amass a wealth of information about these colorful teams and their many talented players. This book, which is the culmination of his decade-long pursuit, represents a singular opportunity to preserve for future generations the important legacy of the Asahi and Zebras. Thus, the Japanese American Museum of San Jose is proud to be the publisher of this monograph which depicts a unique and rich segment of Japanese American history and culture.

Stephen Fugita, Ph.D.
Board of Directors,
Japanese American
Museum of San Jose

PREFACE

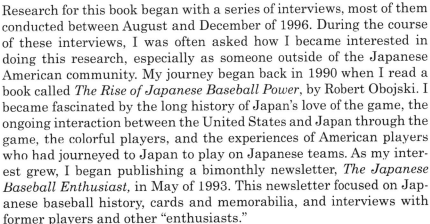

Research for this book began with a series of interviews, most of them conducted between August and December of 1996. During the course of these interviews, I was often asked how I became interested in doing this research, especially as someone outside of the Japanese American community. My journey began back in 1990 when I read a book called *The Rise of Japanese Baseball Power*, by Robert Obojski. I became fascinated by the long history of Japan's love of the game, the ongoing interaction between the United States and Japan through the game, the colorful players, and the experiences of American players who had journeyed to Japan to play on Japanese teams. As my interest grew, I began publishing a bimonthly newsletter, *The Japanese Baseball Enthusiast*, in May of 1993. This newsletter focused on Japanese baseball history, cards and memorabilia, and interviews with former players and other "enthusiasts."

On July 31, 1993, I attended the World Children's Baseball Fair at San Diego's Jack Murphy Stadium, an event hosted by Japanese and American homerun champions Sadaharu Oh and Hank Aaron. As I sat in the stands, I passed out free copies of my newsletter to those sitting near me. One fellow, who had been quietly reading the newsletter for a while, turned to me and said, "You know, my grandfather once got a hit off of Victor Starffin of the Tokyo Giants." I was rather surprised and asked when his grandfather had played in Japan. He said his grandfather wasn't in Japan, but had played against the Tokyo Giants in San Jose, California. I was dumbfounded. "The Tokyo Giants played in San Jose?"

The fellow at the stadium was Jeff Hayamizu and his grandfather was Joe Jio. Several weeks later back in San Jose, Jeff would introduce me to his grandfather and I would begin the first of 28 interviews. I feel very honored and grateful that these players and their families have entrusted me with the preservation of the story of baseball in San Jose's Japanese American community, and I have done my best to share their experiences with you. Thank you all so much!

I would next like to thank the Japanese American Museum of San Jose for their faith in my ability to bring this project to fruition. A very special thank you goes to Steve Fugita, who kindly provided the foreword. Steve, a professor and author, assisted me with most of the

Ralph M. Pearce
San Jose, California

interviews and has provided invaluable assistance since the production of this book began in earnest in December of 2003. Ken Iwagaki has also been very supportive since the early days, doing his best to assist with my many needs. Steve and Ken, along with Roy Matsuzaki and museum president Joe Yasutake formed the subcommittee that recommended the project to the museum board. Thank you all for recognizing the value of this project.

Kenji Taguma and the entire *Nichi Bei Times* staff have been extremely helpful with this project and a large part of this book is due to their very kind cooperation. Besides granting me permission to reprint portions of many of their articles, they provided me with a comfortable place to work, assistance in locating some of the material, and a feeling of being at home in their busy environment.

The Sourisseau Academy of San Jose State has provided funding by way of a very generous grant for which I am deeply indebted. Thank you for supporting this important chapter in the history of San Jose.

Another tremendous thank you goes to Yoichi Nagata, an author and authority on Japanese baseball who lives in Kawasaki, Japan. Yoichi provided the initial encouragement to record the story of the San Jose Asahi, and he has been very helpful over many years providing data, translation, and suggestions.

Several friends from the San Jose Public Library also deserve thanks. Lynn Harris did wonderful, expert analysis of the scorebooks from Japan and provided daily encouragement. June Hayashi helped with many suggestions and edited the initial draft. Computer genius Michael Imada answered many of my software questions. Charlene Duval was very helpful with tips on doing deed searches at the County Recorder's Office. From the California Room my thanks go to Bob Johnson, Lucille Boone, and Judy Strebel for their expert assistance. I would also like to thank Hilary Langhorst, for her sharing her publishing knowledge, and Lorraine Oback for her very thorough and professional handling of publicity for the book and accompanying exhibit.

The multi-talented Bonnie Montgomery cannot be thanked enough as she came to my rescue with her professional editing skills. Bonnie also recommended Cathleen Fortune who did a beautiful job with the cover.

Thanks also go to Dr. Tokio Ishikawa, a lifetime resident and historian of Japantown who was always ready to answer my questions; Jerry Hinaga, who was my host and guide while in Los Angeles and who has provided assistance in so many ways; Kerry Nakagawa of the Nisei Baseball Research Project who has been very supportive and encouraging; Alice Taketa, who trusted me with her wonderful scrapbooks; author Daniel E. Johnson for providing Japanese tour information; author Pat Adachi for her assistance regarding the Vancouver Asahi; Thomas Kurihara for copies of the Asahi's Japan tour scorebooks in which games were meticulously recorded by Thomas's uncle, Earl Tanbara; thanks also to Thomas Kurihara for a copy of the *Keijo Nichinichi Shimbun* that detailed the Asahi's games in Korea;

Michael Santiago for his many hours of intern assistance; and local author John Spalding for his kind advice and encouragement.

Finally, my greatest debt of gratitude goes to my wife Emelie and my son Michael for their patience over the many, many hours of interviews, research and writing.

INTRODUCTION

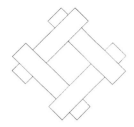

Baseball began its evolution into the modern game from as long ago as the American Revolution, when soldiers in the Continental Army batted balls and ran bases for entertainment during their long encampment at Valley Forge. A blend of informal bat-and-ball games and English cricket, baseball's popularity grew steadily. By 1865, baseball was being widely touted as America's "national game." A few years later and half a world away, the seeds of baseball began to germinate in Japan. The culturally dissimilar Japanese had only twenty-five years earlier opened its doors to the West.

Credited with being first to introduce baseball to the Japanese, American educator, Horace Wilson taught the game to his students at Tokyo University in the early 1870s. In 1873, Albert Bates, a teacher at Kaitaku University, is said to have organized one of the first baseball games in Japan. In 1878, Hiroshi Hiraoka, who had studied in the United States, formed the Shimbashi Athletic Club, Japan's first organized baseball team. The players were said to have worn wooden sandals *(geta)*. In this same period, Englishman F. William Strange wrote the handbook *Outdoor Games* for Japanese schoolboys, in which he devoted most of his attention to baseball. Through these and other influences, baseball began to catch on, but it was a slow process. Throughout the 1880s, baseball was regarded as something of a novelty in Japan.

By the 1890s, ten schools had developed reputable baseball teams, particularly Ichiko (First Higher School of Tokyo). On May 23, 1896, in the historic first official baseball game between American and Japanese teams, Ichiko defeated the condescending Americans of the Yokohama Athletic Club by the score of 29–4. A rematch was played on June 5, with the Americans again losing, this time by the score of 32–9. These victories greatly inspired enthusiasm for baseball in Japan, and beginning with Waseda in 1905, the country began sending university teams on baseball tours of the United States.

The popularity of baseball or *yakyu* (literally "field ball") continued to grow in Japan and by 1930 it began to rival *sumo* (Japanese wrestling) as the national pastime. Over time, baseball has far outdistanced *sumo* as the nation's most popular sport. Baseball's popularity was due to the fact that it was so well suited to Japanese culture. As

"Whoever wants to know the heart and mind of America had better learn baseball..."

Jacques Barzun

1

Donald Roden pointed out in an article for *American Historical Review*, "...baseball in particular, seemed to emphasize precisely those values that were celebrated in the [Japanese] civic rituals of state: order, harmony, perseverance, and self-restraint."

Japanese immigrants first began arriving in the Western United States in the mid-1890s to supplement Chinese agricultural labor. The Japanese were beginning to replace the Chinese who had arrived earlier, but who were being driven out by a statewide anti-Chinese movement.

Many new Japanese immigrants were drawn to California's fertile Santa Clara Valley, where they established a Japantown near the existing Chinatown at the northern city limits of San Jose. Although many Japanese lived in clusters throughout the valley, San Jose's Japantown served as a community center for the business, religious, and social needs of the immigrants. It was during this very early period that the first Japanese American baseball teams began to appear.

The first Japanese American baseball team in California was the Fujii Club of San Francisco, organized by Chiura Obata in 1903. Other early teams included the Oakland Asahi and the Harbor View nine of San Francisco, which was managed by Mr. Komura of the *Stockton Times*. Between 1903 and 1915, many Japanese American baseball teams organized, including teams in Fresno, Florin, Stockton, Sacramento, Lodi, and San Jose. These teams were composed primarily of first-generation immigrants (Issei). Several prominent Issei, such as Frank Fukuda (Pacific Northwest) and Frank Kino (Los Angeles) had played baseball in Japan and contributed greatly to the Japanese American game in the United States. Since baseball did not become popularized in Japan until the 1920s, it appears that the new immigrants' love for the game developed after their arrival to the United States.

California's first baseball team was organized in San Francisco, ten years after the gold rush of 1849. In 1866, the Pacific Base Ball Convention was organized and the following year 25 clubs from San Francisco, Oakland, Santa Clara, and San Jose had joined.

By the time the Issei organized their San Jose Asahi team in the early 1910s, San Jose had a great number of baseball teams. San Jose joined the California State League in 1891, and in 1913 the semi-professional San Jose Bears were entertaining crowds at the city's new Luna Park diamond.

San Jose also had a city league composed of the talented amateur teams of J. S. Williams, Brassy, Label Printers, Winningers, Garden City Wheelmen, and Greystone. Games were played at D & M Diamond at the junction of First and Second Streets and Grant Diamond on Empire Street. High school and college teams, such as Santa Clara College, were well known for their high caliber of play, sending many players to the minor leagues. San Jose also had a grammar school league of eight teams from Horace Mann, Lincoln, Longfellow, Lowell, Hawthorne, Grant, Gardner, and Washington schools.

Baseball in the early 20th century enjoyed a great popularity and received much less competition from other sports or forms of entertainment available today. Whether the Issei became acquainted with the game in Japan or after their arrival to the United States, these first-generation Japanese immigrants came to be known for their insatiable love of baseball. This love would push them to organize and supply teams, build ballparks at home and in relocation camps, and transport teams across the Pacific and back. It would also, perhaps unknowingly, narrow gaps between generations and ease acceptance into a foreign culture.

Chapter 1

BIRTH OF A BASEBALL TEAM

"Well," he says, "why don't you organize a team in San Jose?"

Jiggs Yamada

The story of the San Jose Asahi baseball teams begins with the Issei, the first generation of Japanese who began immigrating to the United States in the mid-1890s. The Issei loved baseball, and they were the ones who established and supported Japanese American baseball before World War II.

The Issei Asahi (ca. 1913–1917)

The earliest evidence of the San Jose Asahi baseball team exists in the form of a photograph taken between 1913 and 1914. The team name "Asahi" (meaning "morning sun") was one of the most popular names for Japanese American teams at the time. Honolulu, Seattle, Vancouver, Hollywood, Sacramento, and Oakland have all had Asahi baseball teams. In most cases, Issei gave their teams Japanese names, in contrast to the later Nisei teams, who tended to use names in English. Very little is known about this team beyond that its players were Issei. It appears to have disbanded by 1917.

One of the players shown in the photograph was Hideichi "Harry" Okida, who was the team's second baseman, according to his daughter Grace (Okida) Kogura. He married in 1917, and by the following year, he was encouraging Nisei in the local community to form a new team.

Born in a village outside Hiroshima on April 1, 1888, Okida immigrated to the United States with his father, Fukuichi, in 1902. By 1908, he and his father were operating a store in Campbell, California, just west of San Jose. The store, on the south side of Campbell Avenue between Central and First Streets, carried groceries and general provisions for local Japanese families. In March 1911, heavy rains flooded their store, and the Okidas moved their business to 201 Jackson Street in San Jose's Japantown. Harry's uncle, Yoneichi Nakamoto, owned a shoe store nearby at 169 Jackson Street. About 1918, the family built a theater that they continue to own, at 587 North Sixth Street. Known as the Japanese Hall or Okida Hall, entertainment included Noh dramas, kabuki, stage plays, and even an acrobatic act from Japan. Later, Japanese movies were shown, often as part of a fundraiser.

Part of Harry Okida's job was to drive out to local Japanese farms to take supply orders. Some time in 1918, Harry encouraged a young farm boy he had met, Harry "Jiggs" Yamada, to reform the Asahi baseball team. Yamada remembered:

> There was one store in San Jose at that time named Okida....The reason I got to know him, was his folks had a wholesale grocery store. He used to come out with a motorcycle out to our farm in Cupertino. "Well," he says, "why don't you organize a team in San Jose?" because he was older than I was, you know....I had players from San Jose that played and then these Japanese college students from Japan that played baseball, they came. So I had a team

The original Asahi team in a studio portrait taken in 1913 or 1914 at the photography studio of S. Imada, 602 North Sixth Street, San Jose. Players identified are Hirata (center), Sugishita (center left), and Harry Okida (bottom right). Collection of Tetsuko Zaima.

there now. These were mostly all grown-ups, except two of the young fellas that were here in San Jose like Hinaga. Hinaga was a couple of years younger than I was, so we were the young guys. (Jiggs Yamada, 10/23/93)

The Issei encouraged and supported baseball as an alternative to other pursuits available to their sons in Japantown. Masuo Akizuki was an Issei who shared the reasons for his involvement with the team: "Gambling was very popular in San Jose Chinatown [adjacent to Japantown] at that time. I became worried seeing so many young men wasting their time and money gambling....In the beginning, only a few people knew about baseball. We didn't have much support at first, but after a year or two, baseball became very popular." (Misawa, 1981, p. 14). Akizuki remembered Asahi team fundraisers at Okida Hall, usually featuring Japanese movies, but also once a stage play produced by members of the community. As the team grew in popularity, community donations continued to support the team. Perhaps the strongest supporters were Fudetaro and Seijiro Horio, brothers born in Japan in the 1870s who had come to the United States in the 1890s seeking their fortunes. Working as partners, by the 1920s they were established, successful farmers. Their love of baseball resulted in their very generous support of the Asahi baseball team for many years.

Harry Okida poses on his late model 1912 Excelsior motorcycle. Collection of Tetsuko Zaima.

Early Years of the Nisei Asahi Team

Although it took a little time, interest in baseball within the Japanese communities really got going with the creation of these first Nisei teams. George Suzuki of the *Nichi Bei Shimbun* wrote in 1941 that "the tempo that brought the Japanese baseball to a new high began in the early twenties when many young players from the Hawaiian Islands were encouraged to come to the mainland to play together with the local Nisei teams organized at that time. During the following five or six years many fine players came to California to put the Japanese baseball on a higher level, thereby enabling various All-Japanese nines to compete with American semi-pro and professional teams." Nisei teams were not limited to Hawaii and California. There were also teams in Oregon and Washington, as far east as Wyoming and Nebraska, Vancouver, Canada, and Tijuana, Mexico.

The Okida Brothers store at 201 Jackson Street in San Jose. From left: Harry Okida's cousin Jitsuo Yamamoto, an unidentified man, Yoneichi Nakamoto, and Harry Okida. Collection of Grace Kogura.

Former Asahi shortstop Chickayoshi "Chick" Hinaga remembered the early San Jose Asahi games, going out to watch his older brother Russell: "The first pick-up team was like my brother, Yamada, Dobashi, Santo, there was a first baseman called Horie...." Those players, plus Jack Kurasaki, a Mr. Takeshita, Henry Kawagoe, Kazuyoshi Uriu, and Tom Sakamoto, made up the 1922 team, the earliest year that news articles have been found for the Asahi. *San Jose Mercury Herald* sportswriter Jack Graham began running a regular column on local baseball that year, and he appears to be the first reporter outside of the Japanese community to mention the San Jose Asahi.

The timing was good for the Asahi, as they were beginning to develop a reputation and a following. Many Asahi players and older members of the Japanese American community remember those games and what they meant to the community. Ex-Asahi player Joe Jio recalled, "Baseball in those days was a big thing among the Japanese communities, because there was nothing else. We played basketball too, but the Issei weren't interested in basketball. I think the only pleasures that the Issei had were going out to the baseball games or to Chinese restaurants. You know, there was no such thing as vacation for them." (8/18/1996).

A portrait of the Asahi's young pitching sensation Russell Hinaga, taken in the late 1910s. Collection of the Hinaga family.

Another player, Frank Shimada, had similar memories: "All the old folks, they supported baseball. Like Jackson Street had benches out by Tosh's Sweet Shop and places like that and they'd be sitting there talking about baseball, especially on Saturday night before the game." (11/22/1996).

Chiyo Ikeda, wife of Asahi player George Ikeda remembered going out to the games: "I was there with the family. I don't know how old I was, but I'd tag along. It was a family event. The farmers would come from the country, Berryessa, Santa Clara, all over and make a day's outing, kids and babies and all." (8/23/1996).

Dr. Tokio Ishikawa was born in 1910 and grew up in Japantown. As a child he was a fan of the Asahi ball team and remembered that when the Asahi went on the road, children would pile onto the back of a large truck and be driven to the neighboring town to see the game. For those left behind, the score would be phoned in and be posted on the brick wall of the Kogura building at Sixth and Jackson Streets. He said that anything newsworthy would be posted there.

Frank Shiraki, former catcher for the Asahi, like so many players from the 1930s, remembers going to see the team play as a youngster in the 1920s: "With the original Asahi team, I remember going to Sodality Park. All the teenagers were really hopped-up about the Asahi. If I remember correctly, they had a certain section that had a cheerleader who used to cheer the team on. These were all Nisei youngsters then." (9/13/1996).

According to ex-Asahi Sumito Horio, the young Nisei weren't necessarily the only loud ones: "I remember one guy was sitting up there, he comes to every game. He tells them, 'Hey, easy guy!' he used to holler, you could hear him. There were a few Nisei, but they were mostly Issei. The Issei really enjoyed watching the games. They worked so hard, so that was their outlet." (8/15/1996).

At least ten Asahi uniform designs were seen between 1913 and 1942. The Asahi weren't overly strict about the uniforms worn, and it wasn't unusual to see a player wearing an older issue. Also, a first year or substitute player might wear a blank jersey. Asahi player Adrian (Onitsuka) Yamamoto described the Asahi uniform: "The Asahi uniforms were red and white; a white uniform with red lettering. The hats didn't matter, any kind of a hat, we wore black mostly. The lettering was all red and the socks had red stripes." (10/27/1996). Yamamoto did not wear the cap that had been issued with his uniform; he preferred a favorite cap that he had acquired on a different team.

Besides the main team, the Asahi also had a "B" team made up of younger players waiting for their chance to join the main team. The Asahi "B" team was strong and often played against the first teams of smaller towns. It appears that the "B" team had a uniform distinct from the main Asahi team.

Sportswriter Jack Graham was very supportive of the team and made an ongoing effort to encourage the entire San Jose community to attend Asahi games and to accept the team into the local baseball scene. Jiggs Yamada said that he was "100% for us." Graham first mentions the Asahi in the *San Jose Mercury Herald* on May 7, 1922:

> The Japanese Asahi and the Fourth Wards will cross bats at the [Asahi] diamond at 2 o'clock this afternoon and fast ball will be in order as the Asahi team has the biggest bunch of rooters behind them of any team in the city; their diamond is probably the best in town and fast games are the rule. The writer wishes to state that anyone wishing to see enthusiastic ball should witness the Japanese team play. Manager Larocca is ready to open for games with any team in the country. Ring him up at San Jose 2679M.

Salvadore Peter Larocca managed the Asahi for a while in 1922 and even served as catcher in a game against the Firemen's team on May 4 of that year. He was a member of the San Jose Fire Department and a resident of Japantown. Dr. Ishikawa remembered that Pete Larocca later umpired many of the Asahi games. He also recalled some of the other *hakujin* (Caucasian) who had helped out with the team: "The Asahi had a *hakujin* coach one time named 'Red' Kerber. He lived on Fifth Street, two houses south of Empire. His little house is still there. They had a black coach [Mr. White]. I don't know his credentials at all....I don't know where he played baseball, but they had him for about a year." (8/15/1996). Red Kerber was a local ballplayer who had played on a number of teams, including Del Monte.

From the beginning, the Asahi team played with and against non-Japanese teams. Dr. Ishikawa recalled some of the local teams and the opportunity that baseball provided for the Japanese to interact with the greater community:

> They played a lot of *hakujin* teams, local teams. They played Garden City Billiards, which is now Garden City.... and they had Consolidated Laundry...then they had two lodges, Woodsmen of the World and Modern Woodsmen of America. Southern Pacific had a team....those were the

teams that they played more games with than against the Japanese teams.

There was no league that I know of...but there were good semi-pro teams. Semi-pro baseball was big in the Bay Area, all kinds of teams in San Francisco and Oakland.

They had fun. They enjoyed the game, the Nisei players, they'd play anybody. I don't think there was any feeling of beating the white guys or anything like that. I think that they were happy to play with them whether they lost or won. There was always a good feeling between the competing teams.

I'm sure that they realized that playing baseball with the *hakujin* was one way of interaction. That was the only way really, unless with their farming business, talking with the produce merchants and people like that. That's strictly business. This was one way you could interact with whites on an even basis. (Dr. Tokio Ishikawa, 8/15/1996)

Frank Shiraki recalled that the team would sometimes use their knowledge of the Japanese language to their advantage: "When we were playing a Caucasian team, we could throw in a little Japanese in there where we figure the Caucasians don't understand...like '*Chicka iku yo*', meaning you're going to throw to Chick." (9/13/1996).

Asahi Diamond, Sixth and Jackson

In the early days of the Asahi, the team played in a lot adjacent to Japantown at the southeast corner of Sixth and Jackson streets. Jack Graham began referring to the lot as the Asahi Diamond. This was an appropriate name for the lot, as it was a full diamond, but it lacked a full field. A full size ballpark was built in 1926 at Sixth and Younger Streets. The newer field was also referred to as Asahi Diamond on occasion, but was officially known as Asahi Baseball Park.

Dr. Ishikawa remembered the old Asahi Diamond well, as he used to watch many ball games there as a child (8/15/1996):

There was an empty lot right next to Garden City Pottery. Garden City Pottery had the whole south half of that block and the north half was empty. That was the only fence for the ballpark. This was the right field fence. Home plate was on the corner of Sixth and Jackson Streets. Right field was shorter; left field went on across Seventh Street. Because of the railroad track and because of the heavy railway traffic due to the cannery being across the street, not only did they have the through trains coming through, but switch trains bringing empty boxes and taking away full boxes...it was too small, actually. They had a grandstand too, you know. The pictures of the sumo tournaments [also held in that lot] show the grandstands and I remember them. So even when the kids went up to play pick-up baseball, the *hakujin* and the Japanese kids together, we played there and never asked permission of anybody. We didn't know who to ask. Until, as far as I know, until the war began. (Dr. Toshio Ishikawa, 8/15/1996)

Once, a player from Stockton named Miyanishi hit the ball to the railroad tracks, whereupon it bounced into the door of an open boxcar giving him a home run and a big laugh from the crowd.

Jiggs Yamada spent all his playing days at the old Asahi diamond, leaving just at the time that the new field was built: "Any ball that went out to right field was a 'two bagger' because of the limited size of the field. But left field was wide open to the cannery. We made the stands as close as we

The San Jose Asahi in about 1922 at the site of the original Asahi Diamond at Sixth and Jackson Streets. Back row, from left: Dr. Ajika Amano, Jack Kanazaki, Mr. Tanizawa, Kichitaro Okagaki, Coach White, Masuo Akizuki, Manager Pete La Rocca. Middle row: Russell Hinaga, Kiyoshi Dobashi, M. Horie, Jack Kurasaki. Front row: Mr. Takeshita, George Santo, Henry Kawagoe, Kazuyoshi Uriu, Jiggs Yamada, Tom Sakamoto. Kanemoto Collection, Kawahara Family Album.

could to the street, so we had a lot of room there. People would think how could those guys play there, but we played a lot of big games. Like from San Francisco, we played the Kennedy Seals, a semi-pro team. And then the Oakland Independent, all former big-leaguers or had tried out for the big leagues." (10/23/1993).

Chick Hinaga played on the old field for a couple of years with the "B" team before moving to the new field: "You know that old diamond, you look at it now from Sixth Street where that railroad track is. You know, it's not too far. But a lot of the guys couldn't hit it over the track. When we said that we had a ball grounds over there, they said 'How can you have a ball ground small like that?' You know in those days, I don't know, maybe the ball was not as lively or what, but there were a few *hakujin* used to hit it over the tracks, but we couldn't. The right field was short, so once in a while we used to knock it over." (12/1996).

The 1924 Asahi Team

By 1924, the Asahi had acquired many fine players and had matured into a strong team with tremendous community support. The team of 1924 was, in Chick Hinaga words, "a real team." Part of what made it so in Chick's opinion was its manager, Henry Yoshihara:

> He was a real manager and anyone that was any good, he used to get them to come to San Jose. In fact, there was a

The San Jose Asahi in about 1924 at Asahi Diamond. From left (back row) Tom Sakamoto, Earl Tanbara, Harry Hashimoto, Mgr. Henry Yoshihara, James Uyemura, Ed Higashi, Mr. Takeshita; (front row) Fred Koba, Jay Nishida, Morio Sera, Jiggs Yamada, Frank Ito, Russell Hinaga. Collection of the Ikeda family.

fellow named Araki. His brother-in-law was a catcher and Araki was a pitcher....Right now, going to Stockton or Isleton is no problem. In those days there were cars all right, but you know how slow they were. But [Yoshihara] would go pick them up most Sunday mornings. He would go up so they could play the afternoon game, see. And then after the game he takes them back. He was a real manager (Chickayoshi Hinaga, 12/1996).

Jiggs Yamada and Russell Hinaga had become the veterans on the 1924 team and its central figures. Jiggs, the captain of the team, was also its catcher, and Russell, the team's primary pitcher, was Yamada's competent and reliable battery mate. Jack Graham lauded the pair's playing skills:

Every baseball lover admires the catching of "Jiggs" Yamada and when an All-Star Winter League team was suggested, Jiggs was the one most mentioned for backstop work. Yamada has a perfect throwing arm and woe be unto the man who tries to steal bases on him....Russell Hinaga, one of the cleverest pitchers in San Jose...has wonderful control and when in good shape...is one of the hardest men to hit that we have. Last season when the Hawaiian team was here, Hinaga amazed the spectators by his skill. That game was one of the greatest ever seen in San Jose, even if the Asahi boys were defeated 0 to 1 (*San Jose Mercury Herald*, 5/2/1924).

The rest of the 1924 lineup included Harry Hashimoto at first, Tom Sakamoto at second, and Stanford players Morio "Duke" Sera at shortstop and Fred Koba at third. In the outfield were Takeshita in right, Frank Ito in center, and U.C. Berkeley student Earl Tanbara in left. James Uyemura and Jay Nishida served as utility players for the 1924 Asahi; Ed Higashi was the team's second catcher.

As a junior, Duke Sera began rooming at the Ishikawa's house and commuting by train to Stanford. Seeing how well this worked, Dr. Ishikawa said that he believed this encouraged his parents' decision to send him to Stanford some years later. Duke also held the distinction of holding the record for the farthest ball hit at the Asahi Diamond.

Earl Tanbara was selected to play on a city all-star team that faced off against the visiting Major League Pittsburgh Pirates in March 1924 at Sodality Park. Earl went one for three times at bat, made his hit count when he was knocked in for a run, and made two nice catches in his right field position. Red Kerber, the former Asahi coach, was the umpire of the game. The San Jose all-star team beat the Pirates 9–5.

Japanese and Japanese Americans, especially before World War II, tended to be comparatively short. But what they lacked in size, they made up for in strong fielding, speed on the base paths, and enthusiastic play. Adrian Yamamoto commented on the shorter players:

> [Asahi player] George Yamaoka was a good catcher. For a small guy, he could sure throw the ball. And Russ was a good pitcher. It was amazing how he could pitch. All those pitchers like Kenso Nushida of Stockton, he was like Russ, about the same size. And the catcher from Fresno, Kenichi Zenimura, he was a good player. (10/27/1996)

Meiji University Meets the Asahi

In 1905, Waseda was the first Japanese university baseball team to tour the United States. Since that time, both countries have regularly extended and accepted invitations from each other. This exchange not only helped to improve play on both sides, but did much to encourage understanding and friendship between the two countries.

The San Jose Asahi team of 1924 was good enough to challenge a touring Japanese university team, and on May 2, 1924, they faced the Meiji University team, one of Japan's "Big Six" universities. The game began on a Friday at 2:30 p.m., at San Jose's Sodality Park. As a preliminary, the Asahi "B" team played a morning game against Watsonville's Japanese team. (San Jose lost 13–2.) The foregone conclusion was that Meiji University

Several members of the visiting Meiji University team in the dugout at San Jose's Sodality Park in 1924. After beating Meiji, the Asahi were invited to tour Japan the following year. Collection of the author.

would walk all over the amateur Asahi team, but that was not the case. The Asahi came on strong and at a pace that was too fast for the visitors. Jack Graham summarized the game:

> Russell Hinaga, pitching ace of the Asahi team, had everything on the ball and some of the big visitors were breaking their backs going after his curves and cutting the air at his mystifying drops. "Red" Kerber and "Sore Foot" Lannin did the umpiring in such a manner that there was never a single protest. (*San Jose Mercury Herald*, 5/4/1924)

Russell struck out nine. Jiggs had a great game not only behind the plate, but also at bat. Jimmie Yoshida, substituting for Tom Sakamoto at second base, had no errors, got two hits, and scored a run on a steal. Fred Koba also had a great game at shortstop with five assists.

As it turned out, the Asahi would be the only team on the Pacific Coast to beat Meiji during their tour. When the Meiji University team returned to Japan, it was decided to extend an invitation to an American team to come to Japan the following year for a series of exhibition games. Because of the San Jose Asahi's win over Meiji, it was decided to invite the San Jose team first. The Asahi accepted and plans began for the Asahi to travel to Japan.

Chapter 2

IN THE LAND OF CHERRY BLOSSOMS

"What the hell are you doing with this bunch here? You're supposed to be studying!"

Duke Sera's uncle to his visiting nephew, as told by Jiggs Yamada

Nisei teams began traveling to Japan as early as 1914, when the Seattle Asahi made the voyage. Other teams to tour Japan included the Hawaiian Asahi, Fresno Athletic Club, and the Los Angeles Nippon.

San Jose's opportunity came in 1925 at the invitation of Meiji University, whose team they had beaten the year before. The timing could not have been better for the Asahi, as several of the players, Jiggs Yamada, Morio "Duke" Sera, Fred Koba, and Earl Tanbara, were all anticipating retiring from the team. They all agreed to stay with the Asahi until their return from Japan.

Meiji University may have provided some funds for tour expenses, although much of the burden was on the team and their Issei supporters. The first obstacle would be the cost of transporting seventeen passengers to and from Japan. Jiggs explained how this was accomplished:

> Well, first, we had to get some way to go to Japan. A boat was the only thing we could get. We happened to have a boy, Earl Tanbara...Tanbara's folks, mother and father, worked for the Dollar Steamship Company family in Piedmont. So when he graduated high school, we had his father talk to Mr. Dollar and ask him if he could do us a favor. He said "Sure, as soon as Earl went to Cal [Berkeley] and graduated, he's got to work for me at the steamship company." They were going to open up an agent in India. So he said, "Sure, if he promises to do that, I can have him going on our boat to Japan."...So that's how we got to go to Japan on a boat. People figured it was funny how we got to go to Japan...because at that time the steamship boat was expensive. (Jiggs Yamada, 10/23/1993)

Asahi supporter Seijiro Horio provided most of the remaining funds for the trip, writing an $800.00 check a few days prior to the team's departure.

Jack Graham publicized the upcoming tour to Japan in a number of articles preceding the trip. On March 18, 1925, the day before the team departed, Graham wrote in the *San Jose Mercury Herald*:

> There will be a big delegation of fans in attendance and a bumper crowd of Japanese fans will be on hand to see their favorite sons in their final game in this city.

> The Asahi team will sail on Saturday for Japan, where they will play a series of games in the flowery kingdom. On their return, they will stop in the Hawaiian Islands, where they will play seven or more games. It will be the latter part of June before they return.

> The Asahi team has made many friends in this city by their gentlemanly manner in playing the national game, and

whenever they stage a game here there is always sure to
be a big turn-out. (*San Jose Mercury Herald*, 3/18/1925)

The following day, Graham ran a column praising the Asahi and encouraging local pride in the Asahi as representatives of San Jose. A large
photograph of the team ran at the top of the sports section, remarkable
in that images of local teams rarely appeared in either American or Japanese American papers at the time. The caption read in part: "The Japanese
Asahi baseball team will leave San Jose on the first leg of its journey to
the land of cherry blossoms this morning, when it takes the train to San
Francisco where it will stay until Saturday, when it will embark on the
President Cleveland for Japan." (*San Jose Mercury Herald*, 3/19/1925).
The article then goes on to identify each of the players in the photograph.
While the team was in Japan, the strong Asahi "B" team continued to play
against teams of their caliber. Asahi Diamond was also made available for
the use of other local teams, and management of the diamond was tempo-
rarily turned over to locals Happy Luke Williams and Chet Maher.

The Asahi, along with manager Kichitaro Okagaki and treasurer Nobukichi Ishikawa, left from San Francisco on March 21, 1925, and a little over
two weeks later they arrived in Japan, giving them about a week to recover
before their first game. When the team arrived, Earl Tanbara purchased
two Mizuno baseball scorebooks. Earl kept meticulous track of each game,
including dates, locations, and names of all the players.

The Asahi played their first game on Saturday, April 11, against Waseda
University, a tough team to face first. Not too surprisingly, the Asahi lost.
They played a decent game however, losing by a score of 12–9. It was something of a slugfest in which the Asahi just could not match. Russell Hinaga
and Jimmy Araki shared the pitching chores, Frank Ito doubled, Harry

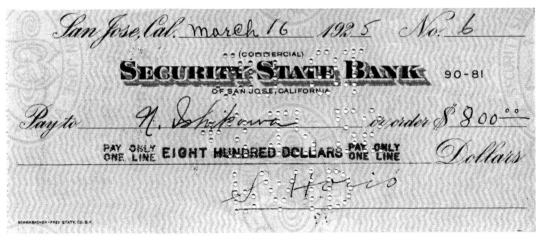

*On March 16, 1925, Asahi supporter Seijiro Horio wrote this $800.00 check to team treasurer Nobukichi
Ishikawa to cover the Asahi's expenses during their tour of Japan. Collection of Ralph Horio.*

Hashimoto tripled, and both Sai Towata and Earl Tanbara hit home runs. Each side recorded only one error.

The Asahi played their second game two days later against their hosts, Meiji University. This time Jimmy Araki pitched the whole game with Ed Higashi catching. Jimmy got knocked around for a 9–4 loss, despite a batch of errors by Meiji.

Next up the following day was Keio University, another tough team. If the Asahi were ready for a win, it would have to wait for another day. Jimmy and Russell teamed up again and received a real shellacking, a 20–4 loss with seven Asahi errors.

Two days later, on April 16, the Asahi faced their fourth team, Tedai Imperial University. Once again Jimmy and Russell teamed up. The boys were playing sharper this day, making only one error. Harry Hashimoto hit two doubles, chalking up their only run in a 6–1 loss. This would be their fourth loss in four games. The Asahi played for the love of the game, but they were serious competitors and this situation was not acceptable. Jiggs explained the problem and the remedy:

> We didn't play so good because our legs were shaking and all that and the ball was different. It was a regular size American ball, but the cowhide, it slips. The pitcher couldn't play, pitch curves or anything and the players themselves couldn't throw the bases, so we couldn't play good. So finally we told the manager of our team, "Get us some American balls." So they sent us a one dozen box of American balls, then we started to play different. Then we started to play our regular play. (Jiggs Yamada, 10/23/1993)

A postcard of the Dollar Steamship Company's President Cleveland, which carried the Asahi to Japan in 1925. Collection of the author.

On April 18, the Asahi played Hosei, yet another strong university nine. Jimmy Araki took to the mound for the Asahi, and despite several errors, the team finally got its first win. The Asahi amassed their total of seven runs in the first three innings, thanks in part to a home run by Araki himself. The final score was 7–4.

The team left Tokyo and headed north to Sendai, where a week later they won a 25–5 victory over the Sendai University team, with Russell pitching and Jimmy sharing left field with Earl. The Asahi traveled 500 miles south to Osaka, where they would suffer another loss on May 1, against Takarazuka University. Their final two games in Osaka began a thirteen-game winning streak. Their next stop, Kyoto, pitted them against the Kyoto Imperial University team, Tom Sakamoto hit a dramatic "sayonara home run," or game-ending home run, in the tenth inning to win a very close game. The Asahi then headed south to Hiroshima for two games.

As the Asahi traveled the country by train, they continued to accumulate wins and, more importantly, became acquainted with the land of their parents. One of the players, Duke Sera, had been born in Hawaii and was raised by his uncle in Hiroshima, who sent him to Stanford University to complete his education. When the team visited Hiroshima, Duke's uncle held a reception for the team. According to Jiggs, when the uncle met Duke and the team he quipped, "What the hell are you doing with this bunch here? You're supposed to be studying!"

After the final game in Hiroshima on May 12, the team traveled roughly 400 miles back to Tokyo. The team originally intended to return to the United States sometime in June. Whatever plans they may have had, however, were altered upon their return to Tokyo:

> In Tokyo, there's a letter to our manager that they want us to go to Korea, because the Korean government, the American Consulate and all that, were anxious to see us play against the Japanese there. It was a lot of fun there, because the American consuls and their families invited us to dinner the night before the game.
>
> In Keijo [now Seoul], the capitol of Korea, they all came out to watch us play. When we played, first we had infield practice and batting practice and all that and you know we talk nothing but English. We don't talk Japanese when we're playing ball. Then this guy, this American guy, says, "Oh boy, we got an American team here, we haven't got a Japanese team!" (Jiggs Yamada, 10/23/1993)

The Asahi played four games in Japanese-occupied Korea between May 16 and May 21. The first two games were played in Seoul, the third game in Daegu, and the final game in Pusan. All transportation to and from Korea had been provided for by the *Asahi Shimbun* newspaper in Japan.

Photographs from the Asahi's game on May 17, 1925, with All Keijo in Japanese-occupied Korea. Published in the now defunct Japanese newspaper Keijo Nichinichi, *Fred Koba is shown at the top crossing the plate after his home run in the third inning. Collection of Thomas Kurihara.*

The games in Korea were covered by the Japanese language newspaper, the *Keijo Nichinichi*, which devoted its greatest coverage to a game that it sponsored on May 17 against the All Keijo team. The translated article reads:

> The game between San Jose and Keijo was played at the Ryu-zan Railroad grounds in the middle of the afternoon of the seventeeth day, with plate umpire Marunaka and base um-pires Ishihara and Suzuki. It was a very fine day. A big crowd

swarmed and got excited over the unprecedented great game. Keijo, an uprising team, won the All Korea Championship last year. On this day, pitcher Takahashi performed well for Keijo and San Jose's Hinaga held Keijo batters in check with his breaking balls. The game went into extra innings. Finally, despite Keijo's good efforts, San Jose batter rallied to score five runs in the twelfth and Keijo lost a close game.

The article goes on to give an inning by inning account of the game, summarizing as follows:

The Keijo team was expected to push San Jose hard, if Takahashi pitched well. As Takahashi had few pitches, we expected that he would be rallied against at some point in the game and that Keijo would be beaten by four or five runs. In other words, San Jose's attack was delayed to the twelfth. That was the reason Keijo luckily fought gamely into the extra innings. But it was clear that San Jose looked stronger than Keijo...Keijo, good at overcoming pinches, played better than it was able to. If persistent Yokoyama had played for the Keijo team, the winner might have been reversed. Keijo batters hit well the fastballs off breaking-baller Hinaga. San Jose was confident to win the game, but they should have brought in a new pitcher in the seventh. It was a costly error [by San Jose] that allowed Hioki to score in the ninth [tying the game]. Pitcher Takahashi pitched superbly, using breaking balls on the outside of the plate; however, he wasn't good with a runner on. It was an unexpectedly close contest for San Jose. It proved that Keijo played well. Keijo is expected to win another Championship this year. Keijo fans in the stands were not broadminded enough to cheer for their overseas countrymen, guests from afar. The San Jose players must have felt sad. The Keijo fans, lacking understanding and moderation, jeered at the San Jose players. Keijo fans betrayed the expectations of San Jose's players who wanted to bring back good impressions of their land and countrymen. (*Keijo Nichinichi*, May 19, 1925, translation by Yoichi Nagata)

The Asahi arranged for their return trip to Tokyo to begin from the southern island of Kyushu. The team was made up of players whose families were from either Kumamoto (on Kyushu) or Hiroshima, so the team's first stop would be Kumamoto. Russell's father had written ahead to family in Kumamoto that Russell would try to visit while in Japan. Jiggs was also from Kumamoto and had written to his uncle and grandparents, whom he had never met. Harry Hashimoto and Fred Koba were also from Kumamoto.

Jiggs told a story about arriving at one of the many stops along the way to Kumamoto. It was common for peddlers to walk along the station platform offering their wares to the passengers sitting inside the trains waiting to depart. A passenger interested in something would open the train window to make the transaction. At one stop, Jiggs and the players sitting near him could hear one of peddlers outside gradually making his way up to them calling out "Sushi! Manju! Sushi! Manju!" When the peddler had come up even with their window, they all looked out and saw that it was Russ! Jiggs said that this was a typical stunt for Russ, describing him as a funny, comical guy.

The Asahi were well treated by the relatives in Kumamoto, who honored them with a reception. From Kumamoto, they traveled north to Matsuyama on the island of Shikoku. After playing two games on Shikoku, they crossed back over to the main island of Honshu to return to Hiroshima, presumably revisiting relatives and playing two games. The second would be their sixth and final loss of the tour, ending their thirteen-game winning streak.

The Asahi in Osaka, Japan, during their 1925 tour. From left, back row: Kichitaro Okagaki, Nobukichi Ishikawa, Jay Nishida, Morio Sera, Harry Hashimoto, Jimmy Araki, Earl Tanbara, Mr. Takeshita, Fred Koba, and two Japanese officials. Front row: Tom Sakamoto, Sai Towata, Jimmie Yoshida, Jiggs Yamada, Frank Ito, Russell Hinaga, Ed Higashi. Kanemoto Collection, Kifune Family Album.

From Hiroshima, they headed south again, back to the southern island of Kyushu. On Kyushu, they would play two games in Fukuoka to begin an eleven-game winning streak. The game played on June 15, against All Montetsu, was remarkable in that, after each team scored one run in the first inning, neither team scored for 10 more innings. This was a real pitchers' duel, with Jimmy Araki going the distance for the Asahi. Finally, in the bottom of the eleventh inning, Fred Koba scored on a hit by Higashi to win the game. After beating the All Fukuoka club on June 16, the Asahi began their trek northward.

The father of one of the players owned a railroad on the northern island of Hokkaido, who made arrangements for the team to play in Sapporo. On their way, the Asahi played two games in Osaka, then two games in Mito, about fifty miles north of Tokyo. Having traveled nearly the entire length of Japan from Fukuoka to Sapporo, the Asahi played two games in Sapporo on July 1 and 2. Then they traveled south to play two games against the Ocean Club in Hakodate. From there they left for Yokohama (just south of Tokyo) and played their final game of the tour on July 9.

It was during this final game in Yokohama that Earl Tanbara hit the series' only grand slam in the fourth inning. Earl's Tokyo relatives later reported that a sign bearing Earl's name was posted near the field commemorating the hit.

The Asahi departed Yokohama for their return voyage to the United States on July 14, deciding not to play in Hawaii after all.

After a shaky start, the team had collected an impressive 32 wins and 6 losses. The Asahi totaled 217 runs for the tour, while allowing only 97 runs. Nearly half of the runs allowed came in the first four games. Their first winning streak included three consecutive shutouts and a no-hitter. The second winning streak featured four shutouts in a row. Jimmy Araki threw a total of seven shutouts, one of which was the no-hitter against Koryo of Hiroshima. Russ Hinaga also did quite well with five shutouts, one of which was a three-hitter. Eight players had collected a total of seventeen home runs, with Earl Tanbara leading the pack with five. Catcher Ed Higashi had the highest batting average at .342. Earl followed at .318 with 40 more at bats.

Home Again

The Asahi arrived back in the United States in early August. The unexpected extensions of their tour and the trips to Korea and Hokkaido had left the team short on money. At the team's request, the Issei community back home sent more money. The team had originally intended to disband upon their return to the United States; however, to pay off the money they had been loaned, the team would continue to play for another six months.

The Asahi played their first post-tour game on August 16, 1925, beating the visiting Alameda Taiiku-Kai 6–4.

On August 30 at Sodality Park, the Asahi played the first of a three-game series against the local San Jose ball team. Although the Asahi lost 6–4, it was an exciting game. Jimmy Araki hit a home run, Takeshita made a tremendous catch in left field, bringing the crowd to its feet, and Sera caught a foul at the left field bleachers. Three errors, however, cost the Asahi the game. Russell Hinaga's younger brother, Chick, filled in for Fred Koba at shortstop. The *San Jose Mercury Herald* (8/31/1925) reported the following day:

> Few who watched "Jiggs" Yamada, plucky little backstop for the Asahi team, perform in yesterday's game against the San Jose team, knew that a few hours before he had been rendered unconscious in an accident that almost cost him his life, and as it was, rendered the top of his head almost bald as a billiard ball.
>
> While working about the pumping plant on his ranch near Cupertino, Yamada leaned too close to the pump gears. The gears caught his hair, and jerked it out with such force that Yamada was thrown violently and rendered unconscious. He found himself little the worse for the experience, except for the loss of his hair, and insisted in going through his program on the diamond in the afternoon.

The second game of the series was played at Asahi Diamond on September 7. It was another exciting, close game, which the Asahi lost 4–2. The balance of the game may have turned on the single error of the game, Fred Koba's bad throw to first base in the seventh inning. Koba had a great day otherwise, with seven assists and five putouts. Jiggs tied the game up in the second inning when he knocked in Duke Sera with a triple to the boxcars on Seventh Street. It would have been a home run, but the fielder ran out into the street, recovering the ball in time to hold Jiggs to third base.

The third and final game of the series took place at Sodality Park on October 5. Jay Nishida, pitching for the Asahi, had previously been used primarily as a utility player. He threw a great game despite a sore arm, allowing only six hits. Takeshita made a perfect throw from left field in the second inning to shut off a run at the plate. Duke Sera blasted one to the far corner of the field and was across the plate long before the ball got there. Jack Graham described it as one of the greatest hits ever seen at Sodality Park. Russ Hinaga, who played right field that day, knocked one to the score board for a triple. The game was exciting from beginning to end, with the Asahi winning by a score of 6–1.

In perhaps the earliest English language article on baseball run by San Francisco's *Nichi Bei Shimbun*, the paper told about the upcoming duel between the Asahi and Fresno ball teams:

The Asahi Baseball team of San Jose will meet the Fresno team for the deciding game next Sunday afternoon, October 25, at 2:30 o'clock. …will in all probability be the most hotly contested game this season, and the outcome is doubtful. It will be the final of a five game series, in which both teams so far have won two games each. It is expected that a crowd of over 2,000 will witness this battle, in which each side will put up a hard fight. For two years these two teams have run neck to neck in the struggle for state supremacy, and this game is expected to decide much.

This year, three teams are evenly matched for the Japanese state championship. Stockton, the third in this triangle, has recently flared up, like a meteor, and nothing seems to stop their succession of victories. (*Nichi Bei Shimbun*, 10/27/1925)

San Jose won the game against Fresno 7–6, thanks to the strong pitching of Jay Nishida and a spectacular game-winning home run in the ninth inning by Harry Hashimoto. Jay also drove in two runs with a triple.

The Asahi now faced the strong Stockton Yamatos for the state championship. The two teams played the first game on Sunday, November 1, with Stockton winning 2–0. Both teams had defeated Fresno and were now tied at two games each in games with each other. The next game would decide the champion for 1925. On November 8, at the Santa Clara College grounds, Stockton won the final game of the series 9–3, in what was sure to have been a hard-fought game.

The season did end with a victory however, with Fresno inviting San Jose to give them one more chance at regaining their former prestige. The teams met at the Fresno grounds on November 15. With Russ Hinaga pitching, the Asahi won by a score of 8–3.

As star shortstop Fred Koba was nearing the end of his tenure with the Asahi, the *Nichi Bei Shimbun* published a piece in which Fred wrote about the importance of good sportsmanship:

The one time objective in all athletic work was to produce a winner, no matter whether the contest was on the playground or in a wrestling ring, and the methods used were not always above question. Today, we stand upon the threshold of a new era, where this very idea stands in the theory at least, as our treasured motto, "Fair Play Always Wins."

If the popularity of any game is to remain as a permanent feature, there should be the presence of sportsmanship and reliability as imponderable things. The best things in athletics can never be attained until the above qualities receive practical consideration, especially in highly organized competitions. The ideals and ethics for "playing the game" all through life should reign supreme.

All players and spectators should be guided in the spirit of true sportsmanship. An athlete should be a true sport, who prefers to lose than to win by unfair or through dishonest tactics. He should be one who is insistent on giving his opponents a square deal; he wants to deserve the victory he wins.

True sportsmanship is the conduct of an individual before, during, and after a contest. Such conducts which are indicative of improper acts should be eliminated. Conduct should be stimulated by a proper motive springing from unselfishness, which is basic, and accompanied by a regenerative emotion. Each individual then becomes responsible for his part in making the athletic world sacred.

Good sportsmanship is a measure, a grading tool, a teaching tool to measure the play-character of an individual or of a group at play. "Character is higher than intellect." (*Nichi Bei Shimbun*, 1/1/1926)

With the new year of 1926, this chapter of Asahi history was drawing to a close. The exciting and successful tour of Japan would be the grand finale of this first wave of Nisei Asahi players. This team had not only provided entertainment for the hard working members of the Japanese community, but it also served as a positive role model for the younger members.

The team was a bridge between the older and younger generations for whom not only was age a barrier, but language and cultural differences as well. Through the game of baseball, an entire family could share a common interest that could bring them closer, whether in victory or defeat.

The Asahi had become a respected and well-liked team in the eyes of the greater community. Their skillful play and friendly demeanor had brought the Japanese and the larger Caucasian communities closer together, giving each an opportunity to interact socially, which encouraged greater understanding and acceptance. Now a younger, second wave of players stood on the sidelines awaiting their moment in the sun.

Chapter 3

FROM SANDLOT TO STADIUM

"Both my father and my uncle loved baseball. My dad even went chasing foul balls. He'd be out there in a suit and tie and sometimes it would go over the fence and he'd go after it!"

Ralph Horio

After the 1925 season, several key players retired from the team: Jiggs Yamada, Duke Sera, Fred Koba, Harry Hashimoto, and Earl Tanbara. The team's Issei supporters planned to fill the gap left by these departing veterans with talent from the "B" team. Among the new players were Kay Miura, Mike "Chitty" Yamada (Jiggs' younger brother), Frank "Blackie" Ichishita, Chick Hinaga, and George "Moon" Ikeda.

Chick Hinaga recalled that "anybody with any kind of talent" was put on the field to test his abilities. Moon Ikeda's father asked Asahi player Jimmie Yoshida to take his son out to the ball field and try him out: "That day, it was hot as heck for practicing and only two of us are playing out there. There was a guy playing batting practice and two of us have to chase [the ball] all over. It was hot as heck, so for a while I sat down along the fence there and rested. Well, after that my dad asked him how I'm going to be. He said 'He's not gonna make no ballplayer, because he's lazy!'" Ikeda proved Yoshida wrong: he would play for over ten years with the Asahi as a well-respected center fielder.

During a 1996 interview, former Asahi third baseman George Hinaga recalled, "When Moon used to buy baseball gloves, he takes all the stuffing out so it's only leather. We'd say, 'What are you doing George? What are you doing?!' He'd do it so he could feel the ball. He sure caught a bunch of balls that way." Moon was also being interviewed that day, and as George told the story, Moon's face lit up and he exclaimed, "I still got that glove! I played center field. I never used to miss a fly! When it gets in there, it stays there!"

Asahi Baseball Park, Seventh and Younger

Coinciding with the birth of this second-wave Nisei team was the decision to build a new ballpark, a full-size stadium with covered grandstands, restrooms, and no passing trains! Although reported as a community effort, it was generally known that the primary financial backing came from brothers Seijiro and Fudetaro Horio. In June 1926, a deed was recorded, transferring ownership of a parcel north of Hedding Street from Joseph and Isabel Clevenger to three young Nisei men: Shigeo "Harry" Hashimoto, Noboru "Russell" Hinaga, and Thomas Tsuruki Sakamoto.

Brothers Fudetaro and Seijiro Horio loved baseball and were two of the Asahi's staunchest supporters. From left are Fudetaro, Seijiro, and Ralph Horio. Collection of Ralph Horio.

The purchase was made under the names of these Nisei because the Alien Land Law of 1920, which strengthened an earlier 1913 law, essentially prohibited Issei from purchasing property. The deed was recorded just a couple of weeks before the stadium was to open, so it appears that the deal had been struck with the sellers months before.

In 1926, Esau Shimizu was ten years old and living on North Tenth Street, several blocks from where the new Asahi Baseball Park was being built at Seventh and Younger Streets. He remembered looking from his home across the open fields to where construction was taking place. Shimizu thought it took about seven or eight months to build. Ralph Horio, son of Fudetaro Horio, remembers watching his father and uncle working on the stadium. Ralph said that he believes that the labor for the construction was supplied by the community.

Opening day was Independence Day, 1926. The *Nichi Bei Shimbun* described the events of the day:

> A monster crowd packed the grandstand of the new San Jose Asahi baseball grounds to its capacity Sunday, July 4, when the Stockton Yamatos defeated the San Jose Asahi Giants to the tune of 8 to 5 in the grand ground-opening game, while the Asahi second team neatly trounced the Palo Alto team by the score of 6 to 4 as a preliminary to the main duel. Airplane stunts, band music, and the ground-opening exercises completed the glorious Fourth-of-July celebration at San Jose's newest and California's best Japanese baseball park, which was built by the combined efforts of the local Asahi supporters.
>
> After thrilling stunts by an airplane that flew over the grounds especially for the benefit of the Japanese fans, the ground-opening ceremony started at noon, with San Jose's Justice of the Police Court Percy O'Connor as pitcher, Chief of Police [John] Black as catcher, and Chief Recorder Dan Flannery at the bat. A representative of the Japanese consulate was to participate in this ceremony, but he was unable to attend. The band rendered the spirit-raising music, and the game to open the $8,000 baseball park started amid cheers from a throng of fifteen hundred spectators composed mostly of Japanese but including a goodly portion of Americans. (*Nichi Bei Shimbun*, 7/6/1926)

Esau Shimizu recalled going to the game that day: "My father took all of us kids to the game, and I remember he gave us 50 cents apiece to spend on any kind of a treat. Of course, getting something like that in those days was really something." (Esau's two younger brothers, Carl and Roy, would become Asahi players themselves a few years before World War II.)

To help pay for the new stadium, Asahi supporters held a benefit presentation on August 27 and 28, 1927, at the old Okida Hall. The *Nichi Bei Shimbun* (8/27/1927) reported that "The first evening will feature a contemporary play, followed by a comedy-drama sprinkled with tears and laughter. Second day will witness similar comedy plays which will conclude the final evening."

Advertising signs in English and Japanese lined the outfield fence at the park, which helped fund the team. Sumito Horio, eldest son of Seijiro Horio, remembered that his father and uncle did a lot of the work soliciting businesses to put up those signs (8/15/1996). In a photo taken from the grandstands in 1927, over thirty signs are visible on the outfield fence, in both English and Japanese, including Tsuruda Co., Kami Co., Fisk Tire, and Blase Bros. Chick Hinaga remembered something unique about one of the signs:

> On top of the left field fence, that fence must have been eight or ten feet high and on top of that was a big sign, an advertising sign. Tsuruda Brothers used to have that *miso* and *shoyu* factory in San Jose. Their ad up there was whoever hits that wins $50. In those days I don't think anybody could hit that far. The best I did was hit on one bounce over the fence. (Chickayoshi Hinaga, 12/1996)

Asahi supporters Seijiro and Fudetaro Horio also took on the responsibility of maintaining Asahi field. Not an easy task, many of the maintenance duties fell to their eldest sons as they came of age. Seijiro's eldest son, Sumito, tells about some of his chores, which he began in about 1931:

> I remember when the Asahi played; I used to drag the field with a Model A Ford. I might have been 12 or 13. We used to line the field, first base line, third base line. I think it was on Fifth Street, you used to go to turn on the water. I remember when the grass would grow tall; they used to leave a sheep in there. There were about three or four sheep and there was a pen there to put them in when the game was on. (Sumito Horio, 8/15/1996)

Fudetaro's eldest son, Ralph Horio, also helped out quite a bit at the park:

> I used to work at the Asahi ballpark together with Sumito.... Every time there'd be a game; I'd be there with a little box selling tickets. There was a little building there, more like a hut. We used to wait for the guy that sold refreshments; we called him the "soda pop man." We couldn't wait for him to come because he always gave us a free drink, usually Nehi. He was a local; I think he had a store in Japantown....

After it got to be a certain time, I'd run across the outfield and jump up on the scoreboard. There was a little space between the fence and the scoreboard. I was exposed, but the ball rarely came out that far. I think there was a ladder to climb up and walk along the ledge of the scoreboard to change the numbers.

I remember they used to have, behind home plate in the stands, the official scorekeeper with a bell. If a team scored two runs, they rang it twice. From the scoreboard sometimes we couldn't really tell how many rings, so when the center fielder would come out you'd holler at him, "How many was that?"

Both my father and my uncle loved baseball, but it was my father [Fudetaro], who took care of most of the business. After the game he paid the bathhouse [where the players would change and bathe] and all that. I remember having the coin box and giving it to him after the game.

My dad even went chasing foul balls. He'd be out there in a suit and tie and sometimes it would go over the fence and he'd go after them!

We used to get a kick out of watching the players when they left the field after the game, because it was all dirt out there.

This image shows a close-up of the Tsuruda Brothers sign on Asahi Park's left field fence.
If any batter hit the round sign hanging above the fence, they would win $50.00.
The character on the sign reads "just right" or "accurate," meaning that is where to aim.
According to Chick Hinaga, no one ever did. Collection of June Kimura.

They would go roaring in their cars from the first base side all the way round the outfield leaving rooster tails of dust flying in the air. They were driving like maniacs! Harry Kanemoto had a 1935 Ford sedan he used to drive. After the games he used to get on that thing and just take off! We used to love to watch him tear out and I mean tear out! (Ralph Horio, 3/7/2004)

Another responsibility of the Issei supporters, was to hire an umpire for home games. For most games, the team would use a single umpire. Joe Jio explained that "In the old days of baseball, the umpire always stood behind the pitcher, because he had to call the base decisions he'd be closer if he was behind the pitcher." (Joe Jio, 8/18/1996). When the home team supplied the umpire, the visiting team sometimes questioned the umpire's impartiality. Joe Jio remembered that once, "We were playing against Stockton or Lodi and we had a regular umpire come out every Sunday, an Italian fellow they called 'Chickie', who lived over on Tenth Street. He made a wrong call and the other team got so mad they chased him around the field! I can still picture him!" (Joe Jio, 8/18/1996).

Northern California Japanese Baseball League

On November 29, 1925, many of the Japanese baseball clubs in California sent representatives to a conference in Sacramento to draw up a constitution for the Northern California Japanese Baseball League (NCJBL). The new league planned two seasons followed by a final series to determine the state champion. Founding league teams were the Alameda Taiiku-Kai, the Fresno Athletic Club, the Sacramento Nippon Baseball Club, the San Jose Asahi Athletic Club, and the Stockton Yamato Baseball Club.

Although the Asahi had participated in the creation of the NCJBL , they did not participate in the inaugural season because the team had lost too many key players. However, by July 15, 1926, the *Nichi Bei Shimbun* reported that the Asahis had "formed a new team out of the remaining members of the old team" and applied for membership in the NCJBL.

In August 1926, the Asahi were admitted into the NCJBL and included in the fall schedule to begin September 5. The strong Stockton Yamatos placed first for the season, Alameda Taiiku-Kai came in second, with San Jose and Fresno tied for third place. Sacramento finished in the cellar. Since Fresno had won the first season, a championship game was played between Fresno and Stockton, with Stockton taking the championship in the best of three games, winning their second championship in a row.

As far as the Asahi were concerned, it was a successful season. They had a brand new, full-size stadium and a new team that had not performed too badly. To celebrate, the Asahi held a social in late November:

The San Jose Asahi Baseball Club, in order to celebrate the successful season which they have enjoyed in the Coast Japanese Baseball League, tendered a party to the younger set of San Jose on Wednesday.

Thomas Sakamoto acted as chairman and opened the party with a speech explaining the purpose of the party. Then Mr. Sakamoto directed the games of the evening which everyone enjoyed. After the games refreshments were served and dancing followed which was enjoyed by everyone. The party ended about 11 o'clock with each member of the party expressing their feelings as to the success of the affair.

The following evening Mr. and Mrs. Yamada invited the baseball players and several of the girls of San Jose to a Thanksgiving dinner. The dinner was enjoyed by everyone and the rest of the evening was devoted to dancing. (*Nichi Bei Shimbun*, 11/30/1926)

For 1927, the last-place Sacramento Nippons withdrew from the NCJBL, prompting a revised schedule. The spring season began April 3 and ended May 22. San Jose was given the week of April 24 off to allow for their game against the visiting Waseda University team from Japan.

This rare shot taken from the Asahi Park grandstands in August of 1927 shows the centerfield scoreboard (with flag) and the great variety of signage advertising local merchants on the outfield fence. Collection of the Japanese American Museum of San Jose, Ishikawa Family.

In league play, San Jose finished in second place with four wins and three losses, winning games from each of the other teams. Stockton once again took first place, Alameda took third place, and Fresno took fourth.

The autumn schedule was formulated in late August and designed to allow Fresno time to return from their most recent tour of Japan. League play was cancelled in September, however, due to insufficient funds.

With no official league play in the 1928 season, the Asahi hosted what was described as the Northern and Central California Championship baseball games on July 3, 4 and 5, with a trophy presented by the *Nichi Bei Shimbun*. The newly organized San Francisco Showa participated in the event, along with Fresno, Alameda, and San Jose. At this time, Jiggs Yamada was listed as a coach for the Asahi.

On July 4, the Alameda Taiiku-Kai upset the confident Fresno aggregation by a score of 5–3. Alameda went on to play San Jose for the championship, while Fresno played against San Francisco for third place. The final games were played on July 5. The *Nichi Bei Shimbun* reported the following day that 1600 fans saw the Asahi win the trophy. Alameda took second place, Fresno third place, and San Francisco fourth.

The following week, the Showa club of San Francisco made plans to obtain use of Ewing Field for another championship series to be held under the auspices of the San Francisco Jitsugyokai. Official invitations were issued to the Stockton Yamatos, the Sacramento Nippons, Alameda Taiiku-Kai, the San Jose Asahi, and the Showa Club. The Jitsugyokai also presented new uniforms to the Showa club players. The games took place on August 11 and 12. The final game was played between Alameda and San Jose, with Alameda winning 13–6. For their success, Alameda won the Jitsugyokai pennant and four silver cups.

Although there was no formal NCJBL season in 1929, the Asahi would still play informally with other Japanese teams. In a two-game series in June, for example, the Asahi triumphed over the Stockton Yamatos in both games. However, to give them a regular schedule of games, the Asahi joined the Santa Clara Valley League for the 1929 season. Jack Graham of the *San Jose Mercury Herald* was the league president and appears to have been the primary organizer.

In an article about one of the Valley League games, Joe Jio is mentioned as a new Asahi member. Joe first "got his feet wet" playing right field in a game in 1926 at the tender age of 16. He probably spent most of his time on the "B" team before coming up in 1929. Joe would go on to become the Asahi lead-off man with his reliable hitting, playing through the 1940 season. In an article about a game between the Asahi and the local Pola team on July 15, 1929, the *Nichi Bei Shimbun* reported, "The game, which is one of the series of the Santa Clara Valley League championship, was featured by a home run and doubles made by Ichishita, pitcher of the Asahis. Jio, a new member in the Asahi, proved his hitting power by scoring the other home run for the Japanese team. He is playing left field position."

The Asahi did extremely well in the 1929 Valley League and played in the championship game on October 6 against the strong Levins team. This game was one of the earliest for George Yoshioka, who was playing right field. George was a dependable fielder who, like Joe Jio, played through the 1940 season. In the championship game against Levins, Chick Hinaga was mentioned as the outstanding figure of the game. Coming up in the bottom of the ninth with two outs, Chick blasted a home run. It kept the Asahi hopes alive, but they just were not able to hang on. Levins won the game 6–4. Chick also had two singles, a triple, and three stolen bases in the game.

Visits from Japanese University Teams

When the Waseda University team arrived in San Francisco in April 1927, the *Nichi Bei Shimbun* gave the team a welcoming banquet. The *Nichi Bei Shimbun* often participated in such events and typically sponsored championship games and provided trophies to the winning teams. Before coming down to San Jose, Waseda split a pair of games with Stanford University. Following the game with the Asahi, the *Nichi Bei Shimbun* provided a summary of the game:

On April 24, 1927, the Waseda University baseball team came to town to play the Asahi. The grandstands at Asahi Park were filled to overflowing as Waseda beat the Asahi in a close contest. Back row, from left, Chick Hinaga, Tom Sakamoto, Kay Miura, "Nurmi" Honda, unknown player, "Blackie" Ichishita, Japanese official, unknown player, "Moon" Ikeda, Waseda player, Mr. Takeshita, Russell Hinaga, Jay Nishida, unknown player. Other Asahi members in this game included Jim Uyemura, Mike Yamada, Ed Higashi, Mr. Hamada, and Mr. Asakura. From the Kanemoto Collection, Mineta Family Album.

...The bleachers and grandstand were packed to capacity, leaving the standing mob exposed to the sun.

The game was called at 2 p.m., with the following batteries: Waseda, Mizukami and Itani; San Jose, Hinaga and Higashi.

The Asahi fans were elated and possessed high hopes of victory when San Jose raked a two-point lead in the first inning. The score was tied in the sixth and stood unmoved until the eighth when Waseda forced in a lone single to lead which lasted till the end of the game and gave them a one point victory. (*Nichi Bei Shimbun*, 4/26/1927)

Waseda won with the final score of 5–4. Long-time Asahi Jim Uyemura helped with the pitching duties that day. Jim was captain and coach of the strong Asahi "B" team for some time. Esau Shimizu remembered him as one of the players who, like Russ Hinaga, was with the team for many years.

In June of 1928, the Asahi readied itself for another visiting team from Japan, this time Keio University. A *Nichi Bei Shimbun* article on June 13, 1928, read in part:

...The Asahi nine, originally one of the strongest Japanese teams of the state, has just been reorganized and fans expect it to come out with flying colors.

The team has only three members remaining of the old "wonder team" who form the backbone of San Jose's strength. They are Tom Sakamoto, Russell Hinaga and Jay Nishida.

These two images were captured from rare footage of Waseda University's game against the Asahi on April 24, 1927, taken by Toshio Kimura of San Jose. In the image on the left, umpire Charley Martinelli removes his mask for the play at the plate as a Waseda player is heading home and Asahi catcher Ed Higashi waits impatiently for the ball. In the image on the right, dust flies as Ed Higashi gets spun toward the camera as the sliding Waseda player crashes into him. Collection of June Kimura.

The Keio University baseball team played at Asahi Park on June 14, 1928. Keio won the contest 5–1. From the Kanemoto Collection, Mineta Family Album.

The pitching burden will be borne by Hinaga, the old-time star twirler, and Ichishita and Asakura. Ichishita was the mainstay of the San Jose High School team, which incidentally won the N.C.B. title. Asakura is a Stanford student and an excellent pitcher.

Nishida and Sakamoto are the catchers.

The infield positions are taken by Tokunaga on first, Takesaka on second, Miura on third and younger Hinaga on short. Takesaka and Tokunaga have been playing with the San Jose State Teachers aggregation, which took the "Triple C" championship. Miura shared honors with Ichishita on San Jose High team, while Hinaga has covered the short patch in A-1 fashion for several seasons.

The outer garden is covered by Asakura, Nagai, Santo, Ikeda and Yoshida, all former high school and college stars.

The game was played on Thursday, June 14, at Asahi Field. Unfortunately, the Asahi were overpowered by Keio's strong pitching. Pitching for Keio that day was Saburo Miyatake, who would one day be elected to the Japanese Baseball Hall of Fame. The Asahi narrowly averted a shutout, with the final score being 5–1.

The 1929 season got going with a visit from the touring Meiji University team. This time Meiji would play a two-game series against the Asahi who had beaten them on their last visit. The team arrived on Thursday, April 18, and was taken on a sight-seeing tour by the Asahi committee on Friday. The first game was played on Saturday, with Meiji winning 10–6. Both teams played brilliantly, but the Asahi made many costly errors. Russ Hinaga was pitching, and he was not having a good day. He was relieved in the seventh inning by Watsonville's great "Tar" Shirachi, who was on loan. Tar had been in the outfield most of the game and when he came in to pitch, Russ took his place in left field. Shirachi held Meiji scoreless for the rest of the game. Jay Nishida did the catching for the Asahi that day. Sai Towata rejoined the Asahi for this game, scoring three runs on a triple.

The second game was played the following day, and this time the Asahi loaded itself with non-Japanese "ringers," players from other local teams. Helping the Asahi that day were outsiders Geno, Fragose, Oliver, Trone and Johnson. With Johnson pitching and Trone catching, the "Asahi" lost by a score of 3–1. Playing in right field for Meiji was Tatsumi Zenimura, cousin of Fresno Athletic Club founder Kenichi Zenimura.

In May 1930, the touring Kwansai University paid a visit and played games with San Jose and Alameda. Playing at Asahi ball grounds, Kwansai won a close game of 11–9 over the Asahi. Blackie Ichishita pitched for the Asahi. Alameda lost their game as well, 8–2.

Dr. Ishikawa remembered this period when Japanese were visiting on a regular basis. The Ken Ying Low he refers to was a popular Chinese restaurant located in Japantown:

> When they'd play Japanese teams here, both teams would go to Ken Ying Low after the game. They'd go over to the bathhouse, take a bath, then go over to Ken Ying Low. They'd open the movable wall partitions, and they'd have a banquet. Both teams would eat together in a friendly sort of way with no animosity. (Dr. Tokio Ishikawa, 8/15/1996)

Bay Region Japanese League

With the apparent dissolution of the NCJBL, plans were announced in March of 1930 to form a new Japanese baseball league to include teams in the San Francisco Bay Area. The *Nichi Bei Shimbun* reported on March 4, 1930, that "For many years an athletic league in the Bay section was an impossibility due to clash of interest among the several organizations. The new baseball league will probably be formed among such well known teams as the Oakland Merritts, Alameda Taiiku-Kai, and Showa Club, with a probability that both the Berkeley team and the San Jose Asahi will join." A Bay Region Japanese League was formed from the teams mentioned, with the exception of Berkeley. The teams began competing in the 1930 spring season. The Asahi won the 1930 Bay Region Japanese League championship.

After the championship, the Asahi then prepared to meet the Gardena Yamatos for a three-game series in San Jose. The two teams met on July 4 and 5. With the battery of Hinaga and Sakamoto, the Asahi won the July 4 contest 4–0. The first game on July 5 featured Ichishita and Sakamoto, with the Asahi winning 6–2. In the second game on July 5, the final in the series, the Asahis won yet again, this time by the score of 10–5. The battery for the final game was Kanemoto and Sheik Uyejo. Harry Kanemoto had recently joined the team, pitching and playing third base. Kay Miura, who had been the old "third sacker," had left the team in early 1929.

In the spring of 1931, the Asahi again saw action in the Bay Region Japanese League. In one game against the Oakland Merritts, Russ Hinaga struck out 14 men. It is during this time that sportswriters begin referring to Russ as a player/manager. The Asahi, perhaps the strongest team in the league, captured the championship once again.

On March 29, 1931, a league constitution was drafted for the new Southern California Japanese Baseball Association. Schedules for A and B divisions were created. Teams making up the league were the Epworth Normans, San Pedro YMA, Gardena Yamatos, Nishi Hongwanji, Hollywood Jays, Hollywood Showa, Oliver Club, Daishi Mission, San Fernando, Crown City Athletic Club, Pasadena Taiyos, and West Los Angeles. Additionally, Hollywood JBC and Long Beach were also interested.

In 1932, two new players joined the Asahi "A" team, Frank Shiraki and Harry Kanemoto's brother "Yo" Kanemoto. Yo began filling in at second base, soon becoming the starter for that position. Yo and Harry would play through 1938. One of Frank Shiraki's first appearances was in a game against Alameda on May 23. Frank pitched that game, getting pounded pretty badly for a 12–8 loss. Frank's real skill was catching, and he would play that position for the Asahi through 1936, though it was not always easy for him to get to the games:

> Before the war, I used to live in Mountain View. In those depression days, my father was farming and the games were usually on Sunday, which for a farmer is a busy day, because they had to harvest the produce for Monday market. I know my father didn't like the idea that on a busy day, for me to be going out to play baseball when the rest of the family had to work. If we weren't busy, why he had no objection.
>
> I remember one time that we were so busy I couldn't commit myself, and Russell Hinaga said, "Hey, you gonna be out to the ballgame Sunday?" I said "No, I can't come out this Sunday, we're so busy and my father just won't go for it." So I remember that day, one of the first generation managers, I don't remember if it was Mr. Kishimoto or Mr. Yano or maybe Mr. [Kichitaro] Okagaki, but one of the in-

fluential people came after me to Mountain View, then my father had to give in. Instead of going in my own car, he took me with his car. The game was just about ready to be started and they opened the gate and we drove all the way around the outfield and right behind the stands, where I changed my clothes. (Frank Shiraki, 9/13/1996)

The Asahi played Japanese and local teams as an "independent" for 1932, with the Bay Region Japanese League out of operation. One of the highlights of the season was a three-game series played against the visiting Hollywood Jays on July 3 and 4. The Asahi won the first game 9–5, the second game 24–3, and the final game 12–5. In the third game, Harry Kanemoto started on the mound, then Frank Shiraki took over, and finally Chick Hinaga pitched in what may have been his only trip to the mound. (Chick once said that he always thought that pitching was easy until he tried it.) In the final game, both Frank Shiraki and Moon Ikeda hit home runs, Harry Kanemoto hit two doubles, and Chick Hinaga hit a triple.

The face and reverse of a pendant presented to Chick Hinaga in 1926, Asahi Park's inaugural year. Given to the author by Chick's son Jerry Hinaga.

For 1933, the Japanese League consisted of Sacramento, Alameda, Stockton, Sacramento, San Jose, and Salinas. The championship for this year was won by Stockton. Jack Graham wrote that the Asahi had not seen much action for 1933, due to a short season.

The Asahi Lose a Friend

Jack Graham, after working 41 years as press foreman for the *San Jose Mercury Herald* retired in 1934 at age 62 to devote himself full time to promoting and writing about baseball. On the evening of May 28, 1934,

Jack Graham sat down at his typewriter to begin an article he would never finish. Having suffered a heart attack the previous week, he suffered another attack this particular evening, stumbling out of his office to the sidewalk on Lightston Alley, where he was found a short time later. This attack proved fatal.

Graham's loss was keenly felt, and the following day messages poured into the *San Jose Mercury Herald* sports department from ballplayers, managers, and city officials. A long list of tributes were published two days later, exemplified by this statement by "Zeke" Ferry, supervisor at Agnew State Hospital and manager of Agnew ball club:

> I have had the pleasure of being associated with Jack for a long time and I considered him one of my best friends. He was a conscientious critic and the best friend amateur baseball ever had. Graham was the best man on the coast in his line of work. He helped more young players to get started than any other man I have ever known. (*San Jose Mercury Herald,* 5/30/1934)

Several memorial tributes were paid to Graham such as these:

> The Flag at Sodality Park was flying at half-mast when the San Jose Bees and the Asahi, Japanese baseball team, played there yesterday. A memorial program including "taps" and a short eulogy will be given when the Bees play on the Asahi diamond Sunday afternoon. Black arm bands will be added to the Bees' uniforms.

> The bouts in Forman's arena Tuesday night were interrupted while followers of this sport paid tribute to Graham. With the lights out Timekeeper Bob Rotholtz sounded "ten" upon the gong. (*San Jose Mercury Herald,* 5/31/1934)

A year later, on May 17, 1935, the City of San Jose opened a baseball stadium dedicated to the memory of Jack Graham. At the dedication ceremony, Jack's son Malcolm placed a memorial plaque on its pedestal which read:

GRAHAM FIELD
Dedicated to the Memory of
JACK GRAHAM
1872–1934
Father of Sandlot Baseball of Santa Clara Valley

Located on Willow Street, the field was lighted for night games; the grandstands were expanded in 1938 from 1200 to 1450 seats. The grandstands burnt down in October of 1947 through an act of juvenile vandalism. The land was then subdivided with the addition of a new street named Graham Avenue.

The San Jose Asahi had lost a real friend in Jack Graham. From his earliest articles in 1922, Graham not only wrote about the Asahi in depth, introducing the players and reporting on games in detail, but he encouraged acceptance and interaction between the Japanese and the greater community.

Revival of the Northern California Japanese Baseball League

Shortly before his death, Jack Graham wrote, "After a long time in seclusion, the Asahi ball team has reorganized and will have an exceptionally strong club this season." (*San Jose Mercury Herald*, 3/25/34). The reorganization included the revival of the NCJBL, which consisted of San Jose, Alameda, Stockton, Sacramento, Salinas, and Fresno.

New to the team this year was Jack Ota, who later changed his last name to Fujino. Jack would become a back-up catcher behind Frank Shiraki. This would be especially useful for times when Frank had trouble getting time off for the games. Jack tells about joining the team:

> I graduated high school in 1931 and I tried to latch on to these American teams. After I got a little experience playing against the Caucasian guys, I figured I might be good enough to try to join the Asahi ball team. I did and played for quite a few years. Of all the teams in this area, I think San Jose was one of the strongest of all the Japanese teams. (Jack Fujino, 8/22/1996)

The Asahi won the first half of 1934 season and also beat Lodi, who was the winner of the Sacramento Valley League. In the deciding game for the second half championship, San Jose faced Stockton. In the seventh inning, with Stockton leading 1–0, San Jose walked off the field in a dispute over the umpire's decision on a close play at home plate. This gave the second half championship to Stockton. No title game was played, so San Jose and Stockton became co-champions for the year.

The Asahi had experienced many shining moments in their many years of play: the tour of Japan in 1925, the construction of their own ballpark in 1926, and championship seasons in 1930, 1931, and 1934. What would perhaps be their finest moment lay just ahead.

Chapter 4

TOKYO GIANTS COME TO TOWN

"I remember the
Tokyo Giants were going
to come and Russell
was going to pitch.
My uncle used to take me
to where he was working
and play catch so he
could warm up his arm.
This was about three or four
times a week."

Sumito Horio

Besides the frequent exchange of university teams between Japan and the United States, professional teams from the United States had also been touring Japan as early as 1908. Although the Japanese loved baseball, and games against professional touring teams from the United States were very popular, the Japanese public was not yet sold on the idea of rooting for Japanese professional teams. (Three professional teams organized in the early 1920s, but none survived more than a few years.) Matsutaro Shoriki, head of the Tokyo-based newspaper *Yomiuri Shimbun*, had a tremendous desire to see professional baseball succeed in Japan. After a very successful tour by major league stars in 1931, Shoriki decided that he would build a team of the best Japanese players he could find to face the next team of major league players that toured Japan.

The most recent major league tours had been organized by Herb Hunter, who brought the best players of his day to not only play against, but give instruction to the Japanese, who were described as very eager students. Major leaguer Lefty O'Doul, who had participated in the tours of 1931 and 1932, assisted Matsutaro Shoriki in convincing the great Babe Ruth to make his first trip to Japan for the next tour.

Babe Ruth and Company Tour Japan

The American League Stars set sail for Japan in October 1934. The team was led by the venerable Connie Mack, manager of the Philadelphia Athletics, with Babe Ruth acting as team manager. Other big names in the tour included Lou Gehrig, Charlie Gehringer, Earl Averill, Jimmie Foxx, Lefty

Victor Starffin on an early 1950s Japanese baseball card. Elected to the Japanese Baseball Hall of Fame in 1960, Starffin accumulated a lifetime record of 303 wins (the sixth highest) and still holds the single-season record of 42 wins, set in 1939. Collection of the author.

Gomez, Lefty O'Doul, and Moe Berg. When the American League Stars arrived in Yokohama on November 2, 1934, they received a tremendous reception. Parading down the Ginza in open cars, thousands of spectators caught a glimpse of the famous Babe Ruth. These major leaguers made a lasting impression on the Japanese, not only with the high caliber of their play, but also with their efforts to please the fans. On one occasion, they played an entire game in the rain. Early in the game, a fan came onto the field to offer Babe Ruth an umbrella at first base. Ruth did not really want it, but accepted it and played the entire game holding it! Other players also got in on the act, when Gehrig was loaned a pair of goulashes.

Shoriki worked hard to organize the All Nippon team to face the Americans. Eleven of the players on All Nippon were future Japanese Baseball Hall of Fame inductees, including two pitchers, Eiji Sawamura and Victor Starffin.

Eiji Sawamura was elected to the Japanese Hall of Fame in its inaugural year of 1959. Sawamura gained legend status by holding the American League Stars to a single run on November 20, 1934. All Nippon lost the game 1–0, but the Japanese were greatly encouraged by this feat. The Sawamura Award is given annually to Japan's most deserving pitcher and is equivalent to our Cy Young Award.

Victor Starffin was not of Japanese ancestry, but he came to Japan as an infant. Starffin's father had been a military officer attending Czar Nicholas II and had fled Russia during the Russian Revolution in 1917. Japan admitted the Starffin family as refugees, and they finally settled in the northern city of Asahikawa in September of 1925.

Starffin reached the height of six feet by the time he was 12 years old and began developing his pitching ability while in elementary school. He joined the All Nippon late in the series against the American team and appeared only once, as a relief pitcher. Starffin would go on to become the first 200 game winner in Japan in 1946, reaching 300 wins by 1955. He would retire with a total of 303 wins, 175 losses, and was elected to the Japanese Hall of Fame in 1960.

Another member of the All Nippon team was a Hawaiian, Fumito "Jimmy" Horio. By the time Jimmy joined the All Nippons, he had played on several teams in the United States including the Los Angeles Nippons and the Sioux Fall Canaries of South Dakota.

During their month in Japan, the American League Stars played a total of sixteen games, winning all of them. Fifteen games were played against the All Nippon team and one game against the Tokyo Club. Two additional games were played with combined American and Japanese teams. The Americans outscored their opponents 193 to 42. The scores didn't matter to the Japanese. They never considered the possibility that they might actually challenge this amazing team of professionals.

The 1936 Tokyo Giants on board their ship heading to the United States for their second tour. Among the many talented players on the team are pitching stars Eiji Sawamura (back row, far left) and Victor Starffin (back row, third from left). Collection of Nisei Baseball Research Project / James Tominaga.

Tokyo Giants Tour the United States

Following the American League Star's departure in December of 1934, Matsutaro Shoriki created a professional baseball team with 17 members of the All Nippon team. On December 26, 1934, the Dai Nippon Tokyo Yakyu Club was born, and Shoriki announced his intentions of sending the team on an extended tour of the United States. Before the team arrived in the United States, they had already received the nickname "Tokyo Giants" by Lefty O'Doul, who had been retained as the team's advisor.

Shoriki's team arrived in the United States on February 27, 1935, accompanied by Herb Hunter, who by that time was considered our baseball ambassador to Japan. Under the management of Satoro Suzuki, this team included Victor Starffin, Eiji Sawamura, Jimmy Horio, and many future stars like second baseman Takeo Tabe, shortstop Hisanori Karita, third baseman Shigeru Mizuhara, and left fielder Nobuaki Nidegawa, who along with Starffin and Sawamura, were all future Hall of Fame inductees.

In the month before the Tokyo Giants faced the San Jose Asahi, the Giants split a two-game series against the Missions of Marysville, California, played a four-game series with Sacramento, and lost two of a three-game series to the San Francisco Seals. The San Jose game was set for March 27, 1935. To get Russell Hinaga's arm ready for the game, Fudetaro Horio would drive his 17-year-old nephew Sumito out to play catch with Hinaga about three or four times a week. The day of the game, the *San Jose Mercury Herald* ran a photo of the Tokyo Giants with the following announcement:

> The Tokyo Giants from Japan, shown in the above picture, will go against the San Jose Japanese team here this afternoon at 2:30 o'clock [sic] at Asahi park at the northern edge of the city. The Giants are rated as one of the best professional clubs in the orient, while the local squad is listed among the "big three" of Japanese baseball on the Pacific coast. To encourage baseball interest among boys of student ages, the club has set their admission at half of the regular gate charges. (*San Jose Mercury Herald*, 3/27/1935)

The lineup for the Asahi that day was Russell Hinaga (pitcher), Frank Shiraki (catcher), Blackie Ichishita (first base), Yo Kanemoto (second base), Chick Hinaga (shortstop), Harry Kanemoto and Ky Miyamoto (third base), George Yoshioka and Adrian Onitsuka (right field), Moon Ikeda (center field), and Joe Jio (left field). Ky Miyamoto of the famous Miyamoto clan was on loan from Monterey. In reserve were Jack Ota and pitcher Lefty Mochizuki.

As part of the pre-game ceremonies, the Giants formed a line across the pitcher's mound, removed their caps, and bowed to the grandstand. The Asahi presented the Giants with a silver cup as a memento of their visit. Henry Honda, who had not yet joined the Asahi, watched the game from the stands. He recalled that a loudspeaker was set up especially for this game, with announcements made in Japanese. Catcher Frank Shiraki recalled, "When the Tokyo Giants came the first time, the whole family, even my mother and sisters that didn't understand baseball too much, they called it a holiday and the whole family came." (Frank Shiraki, 9/13/1996).

Pitching for the Giants that day was Victor Starffin. All of the former Asahi who played against the Giants that day remembered the impression the tall Russian had made on them. Grimacing, Moon Ikeda also recalled the impression Starffin had left after hitting him in the arm with a fastball. The game was umpired by Dewey Bowen and scored by former Asahi Tom Sakamoto. Attendance was reported at an estimated 1,000.

The Giants were up first and as each batter approached the plate, they would remove their cap and bow to the umpire as a show of respect. Russell proceeded to shut them down with no hits. The first man up for the Asahi was their regular lead-off man, Joe Jio. Starffin returned the favor and put the Asahi down in order: Joe Jio, Yo Kanemoto, and then Chick Hinaga.

In the second inning, the Giants came out swinging, connecting for two hits and scoring the first run. When the Asahi came up for their half of the inning, they were again put down in order: Ichishita, Yoshioka, then Ikeda.

When the Giants came up in the third inning, they again found it tough going and retired with no hits. Harry Kanemoto was first up for the Asahi, but he had no luck. Frank Shiraki was next up and with a keen eye, drew a walk, becoming the Asahi's first man on base. Following Shiraki was Russ Hinaga, who made a sacrifice hit to move Shiraki to second base. Shiraki was now in a position to score on a decent hit. The next man up was Joe Jio, who recalled, "I remember the hit, it was a cheap hit, what they call a Texas leaguer." That "cheap hit" was all that was needed to bring Shiraki home. With their first hit and first run, the Asahi had tied the game back up with the Giants. Yo Kanemoto made the third out to end the inning.

Russell held the Giants hitless once again in the fourth inning. Starffin was also going strong, putting the Asahi down in order: Chick Hinaga, Ichishita, then Yoshioka.

In the fifth inning, the Giants put together a couple of hits, but they went nowhere. Starffin once again retired the Asahi in order: Ikeda, Harry Kanemoto, then Shiraki.

Russell was holding up well, but in the sixth inning, the Giants were able to muster another run, going ahead of the Asahi 2–1. Russ and Joe gave the Asahi their next two outs, but Yo Kanemoto and Chick Hinaga let the Giants know that they could hit. With two men on, Blackie Ichishita was up. Ichishita was an excellent hitter but had no luck this time and provided the out that would end the drive.

When the Giants came up in the seventh inning, they found the Asahi still able to handle them and again went down hitless. Though Russ would have a total of only three strikeouts for the game, the Giants did not hit well off him. On top of that, the Asahi fielding had been nearly perfect, with only a single error. One of the finest fielding plays of the game was made this inning when shortstop Chick Hinaga robbed Eguchi of a hit by making a high, leaping catch. Unfortunately, the Asahi fared no better in the bottom of the seventh, also going down hitless. Starffin was proving extremely difficult, working his way to a total of 13 strikeouts for the game. The Giants had also recorded but a single error.

The Giants made an attempt to gain some ground in the eighth inning, getting two hits off Russ, but the Asahi continued to hold them and no runs were scored. Although Starffin was now occasionally walking a man, the Asahi remained hitless with Chick Hinaga making the last out of the inning.

In the ninth inning, the Giants batters once again faced the tireless veteran, Russell Hinaga. Even after nine innings, Russell was going strong and allowing a single hit, held off the Giants' attack yet again. With the score still 2–1 in favor of the Giants, it was doubtful that the Asahi could make something happen in the bottom of the ninth with the way things had been going.

Ky Miyamoto was sent in to pinch hit for Blackie Ichishita, a strong hitter who, like most of the guys, was having trouble with Starffin that day. Miyamoto, in his only at bat for the day, pleased the crowd with a clean hit to left field for a single.

The next batter scheduled was George Yoshioka, another hard hitter who was also zero for three attempts against Starffin. Adrian Onitsuka was sent in to pinch hit for Yoshioka and earned a walk, sending Miyamoto to second. Moon Ikeda then came up and took one of Starffin's blazing fastballs on the arm. It was good for a walk, and now the bases were loaded, with Miyamoto's eyes on home plate for the tying run.

With no outs, Harry Kanemoto came up to the plate with instructions to bunt. Harry was not able to put one down, but on his last try, the Giants' catcher Uchibori was not able to hang onto the ball. Miyamoto, with a big lead off third, was able to steal home. (It helped that Uchibori tagged the plate instead of Miyamoto, mistakenly thinking that the play was a force.) The score was now tied, and Adrian Onitsuka was hugging third. The next up was the catcher, Frank Shiraki. Frank had a keen eye and could really belt the ball, but not today:

> My sister was recalling a few years ago, when I struck out,
> that some fan yelled "*Bakatare ga!*" [stupid, foolish]. My
> mother heard that and said, "Why do they say things like
> that?" My sister was telling my mother, "Well, that's all in
> baseball, mom." Then my mother said, "But why are they
> so harsh?" (Frank Shiraki, 9/13/1996)

His strikeout would make two outs in the bottom of the ninth against the pitching of Starffin, who had allowed only four hits all game. The Asahi needed someone now who could seize this slight chance of victory, but the next man to step up to the plate was Russ Hinaga, the smallest player on the team. He too had gone hitless against Starffin in three previous attempts. Reporting for the *San Jose Mercury Herald*, August G. Kettman described what happened next:

> Starffin blazed a strike across the rubber while Hinaga
> watched unmoving. The fans saw only an extra inning
> when the Giants would again get to the gallant little pitcher for the winning runs. The second pitch Umpire Dewey
> Bowen called a ball.

> Starffin wound up for another fast one as little Hinaga, with
> do-or-die determination, choked his bat. The horsehide came
> from Starffin's hand like a bullet and Hinaga, swinging desperately, drove it through second, bringing Onitsuka across
> with the winning run, as the local Japanese colony rushed
> onto the field to hail their hero pitcher who won his own ball
> game. (*San Jose Mercury Herald*, 3/28/1935)

The game, which had taken just a little more than two hours to play, was over. Watching from the stands, Henry Honda recalled seeing Frank Shiraki, in particular, jumping up and down in celebration:

> I remember real well in the bottom of the ninth inning, with a runner on third, Russell Hinaga came up there and got a base hit and scored the winning run. We beat the Tokyo Giants! Boy, what a thrill! (Henry Honda, 5/21/1998)

This was perhaps the Asahi's finest hour; a very difficult game against one of their strongest opponents, dramatically won for a stadium filled to capacity with hopeful fans. Statistically, the Giants appear to have been the stronger team, but there is more to baseball than just statistics.

That evening, the Asahi hosted a banquet for the visiting Giants at the Italian Hotel, a short walk from the DeAnza Hotel where the Giants were staying. Dick Nishimura was the toastmaster and two of the Issei supporters, Mr. S. Oshio and Mr. Kohei Kogura, spoke. Satoro Suzuki responded for the Giants. It was probably at this time that the Asahi presented the game-winning ball to the men who had perhaps made the greatest contributions to their team, Issei supporters Fudetaro and Seijiro Horio. The ball had been signed by the members of the Tokyo Giants, as well as the winning battery, Russ Hinaga and Frank Shiraki. Lost for many years in a

Ralph Horio found this historic baseball by chance in a bag of baseballs in a closet. Although barely legible, one can still make out the inscription: "Last Ball, 3–2, 3-27-35." The ball is signed by the winning battery, Russell Hinaga and Frank Shiraki, as well as most of the Tokyo Giants team. Collection of Ralph Horio.

bag of baseballs, Ralph Horio, son of Fudetaro Horio, found the game-winning ball while this book was being written.

After playing the Asahi, the Giants headed south. Playing teams along the way, they crossed the border into Mexico to beat the Mexicali All-Stars. The Giants then played their way back up through California into Oregon and Washington. From there they would begin an eastward swing across the Rockies. In Detroit, they were paraded through the city before beating the Ford Motor Company nine 6–0. From Michigan the Giants trekked through Wisconsin, then across the border into Canada for games in Winnepeg, Regina, and Edmonton. After winning all of their games in Canada, the Giants headed back to San Francisco for a final victory, winning against a pick-up team organized by the great Ty Cobb. (Cobb himself had traveled to Japan in 1929 on one of Herb Hunter's instructional tours.)

The following day the Giants boarded the Taiyo for Honolulu. In Hawaii they would play five more games before returning to Japan on the Chichibu Maru. The Tokyo Giants had played a total of 110 games, winning 75 and tying 1 for a winning percentage of .687. The San Jose Asahi and the Los Angeles Nippons were the only two Nisei teams to beat them.

Having gained great notoriety, the Giants continued touring in Japan. On December 20, 1935, Japan's second professional ball club, the Osaka Tigers, was formed. In the next few months, many more teams would be organized, and the year 1936 would see the formation of Japan's professional baseball league, with seven teams.

Tokyo Giants Return

Before the inaugural season of 1936 began, the Tokyo Giants decided to return to the United States for a second tour. Arriving in San Francisco on the Chichibu Maru, the Giants began a three-month tour of California, Arizona, Texas, Utah, Washington, and British Columbia. Jimmy Horio did not join the team for this tour. Having spent time with the Pacific Coast League's Sacramento Solons the previous year, he was playing with the Seattle Indians in 1936. Interestingly, he only played three games with the Indians, all of which were against the visiting Tokyo Giants. After leaving the Indians, Horio joined the Hankyu team in Japan's new professional baseball league.

The Giants first game was played against Lefty O'Doul's San Francisco Seals on March 1, 1936. With Sawamura pitching, the Giants beat the Seals 5–0. Sawamura struck out ten of the Seals and allowed only two runs before a crowd of 4,000.

Their second game was played Monday, March 2, 1936, against the San Jose Asahi. The starting pitcher was George Ichishita, younger brother of Blackie Ichishita, with Frank Shiraki doing the catching for the Asahi. For the Giants, Natafuku went the first five innings and Starffin played the last four.

The Giants would score first in the third inning when Kura walked, stole second, and scored on Blackie's error at first with a ball that was hit hard by Tsutsui.

In the fifth inning, Moon Ikeda drove a long triple into left field and scored on Blackie's single. The Giants took the lead again in the sixth inning when Nakajima was safe on a fielder's choice, stole second, and then scored on Hayashi's single. The Asahi tied it back up again in the seventh when Shiraki got an infield hit, stole second, went to third on George Ichishita's single, and then scored on Joe Jio's liner.

George Ichishita did extremely well in another hard-fought game with the Giants, but was pulled in the ninth with one out after walking two batters. Replacing him with runners on first and third was Russell Hinaga. Russ caught Tsuda off base at third for the second out, but then walked the next batter, Kura. Now, in the bottom of the ninth, with the score tied 2–2 and runners on base, Victor Starffin came up to bat against Russell. Starffin connected with one of Russ's pitches for a single which scored Nakazawa and won the game. As had happened the previous year, the winning pitcher batted in the winning run, although the Asahi's fortunes were reversed. It wasn't another victory, but it was another exciting, well-played ball game, which is what the Asahi were all about.

Baseball in Japan after Pearl Harbor

This would be the Giants' last tour prior to World War II. Professional baseball continued to flourish in Japan. Except for 1945, when the war was at its most critical stage for the Japanese, baseball was played in Japan through World War II. During the war years, the Roman alphabet was no longer used and neither were English terms like *sutoraiku* (strike), *pitcha* (pitcher), or *batta* (batter). Victor Starffin, despite his fame as a Tokyo Giant, was forced to change his name to a Japanese one (Hiroshi Suda) and eventually was placed in a detention camp.

Lefty O'Doul made a famous goodwill tour with the San Francisco Seals in 1949. The tour was very significant to the Japanese, and O'Doul was highly praised by General MacArthur. O'Doul was very happy to finally return to Japan, but he was also saddened by the toll that the war had taken on the country and its people and by the loss of many of his friends. One of the greatest players lost was Eiji Sawamura, who was killed when his troop transport ship was torpedoed in December of 1944.

In 1950, a two-league system was created with the championship teams from each league playing in the Japan Series each year. Teams, with names like the Dragons, the Carp, the Whales, or the Swallows, often carry their corporate sponsors name as well. The Tokyo Giants, for example, eventually became known as the Yomiuri Giants (*kyojin* in Japanese), named for the Yomiuri newspaper company that owns them. Though the Tokyo Giants have fashioned themselves in name and uniform after the New York Giants, they have been referred to as the "Yankees of Japan" for their ability to attract star players and win 31 pennants in their first 70 years.

Chapter 5

THE
THIRD
WAVE

"They were heroes,
especially Russell.
He had a kind of
personality that attracted
people to him.
He was small, but he could
play and he could play
forever. He could pitch,
he could catch, and
he could play any place."

Dr. Tokio Ishikawa

With the arrival of George Hinaga, George Ichishita, and Sumito Horio to the senior Asahi team in 1936, the third wave of Asahi players began to arrive on the scene. Jack (Ota) Fujino took over catching for Frank Shiraki that year, and the following season would be Moon Ikeda's last. The players who had formed the second wave were seasoned veterans now, and many were retiring, a phenomenon repeating itself across the NCJBL. George Suzuki observed in 1941 that "By 1935, many old players retired. In their place appeared new Nisei players. With the close of the 1940 season, baseball again appeared well on its way to enjoy the glory of former years." (*Nichi Bei Shimbun*, 1/1/1941).

Two months after the Tokyo Giants' second visit, the Asahi played the touring Waseda University team on May 17, 1936, at Asahi Park. Old timers Russ and Chick Hinaga, Blackie Ichishita, and Moon Ikeda had all played against Waseda during their last visit in 1927. Rookie George Ichishita was the starting pitcher for the Asahi. Holding Waseda to three runs, George got in trouble in the sixth inning, allowing five more runs. Russ came in to relieve George and gave up only two more hits and one

This is the San Jose Asahi as they appeared in about 1936 at Asahi Park.
Back row, from left, George Ichishita, Harry Yoshioka, Jack Fujino, George Yoshioka,
Harry Kanemoto, Sumito Horio; Front row, Joe Jio, Adrian Onitsuka, Yo Kanemoto,
Russell Hinaga, Chick Hinaga, Frank Ichishita, George Hinaga.
The Kanemoto Collection, Kawakami Family Album.

run. Although the Asahi out-hit Waseda 11–10, they lost 9–4, due in large part to sloppy fielding. The Asahi chalked up seven errors for the day.

Joe Jio, George Yoshioka, Jack Fujino, and Adrian Onitsuka supplied the hitting power with two hits each. "I hit a home run in the Waseda game," Jack Fujino recalled. "I think I hit it to center field and it must have gone through his legs or over his head, I don't know which. It was an 'in the park' home run."

A local dentist, Dr. George Isamu Kawamura, stood with the team in a photograph taken just before the start of the game with Waseda. Frank Shiraki said that it was about this time that Dr. Kawamura took over general management of the team. Also playing in the game that day was rookie Sumito Horio, who described himself as more of a substitute player rather than a regular. Even though he was never issued an Asahi uniform, he was a reliable player for several years.

Although the Asahi lost their games with the touring Japanese teams this year, they won the 1936 NCJBL championship against the 1935 champion Alameda Taiiku-Kai. In the ninth inning of the deciding game against Alameda, the trailing Asahis made their final effort. George Hinaga drove in the winning run giving the Asahi a 13–12 win. Harry Kanemoto was credited for his fine relief pitching and Joe Jio led his teammates in hitting.

After league play was over, the Asahi would periodically travel to Los Angeles for games with one of the many strong Southern California teams. One of the teams that the Asahi played many times over the years was the Los Angeles Nippons. Frank Shiraki remembered one of those games played towards the end of his career:

> One time in 1936 or 1937, we went to play the L.A. Nippons. Nowadays it only takes six or seven hours to get there, but in those days, it must have been a ten to twelve hour drive. Luckily, we beat the Nippons. I don't remember what the score was, but both Chick Hinaga and I got home runs.
>
> In those days, they used to have a Japanese movie house in Japantown called Okida Hall. Being that all the Valley knew the Asahi team went to play the L.A. Nips, they announced the score that night at the Japanese hall "...Chick Hinaga and Frank Shiraki hit home runs." Years afterwards an old timer was telling me about it. (Frank Shiraki, 9/13/1996)

Jack Fujino, who had also played for a while with Guadalupe, recalled a trip he made with the Asahi to play against the strong San Pedro Skippers:

> When I was in Guadalupe, we played the San Pedro Skippers. San Pedro was supposed to be one of the strongest teams in California at the time. And so I played in San Pedro and it was Labor Day and we got beat.

A couple of weeks later, I got a letter from San Jose. Russell Hinaga wrote, "Could you help us out? We're going to go play San Pedro." So I wrote back "It's okay, I'll go with you guys."

So we went down there. They won the cup when they beat Guadalupe and when we were just about ready to start the game, they paraded it around. I guess they thought it was going to be a cinch to beat us. They told us they were going to have a banquet after the game and where we were going to go to shower and everything after.

Well anyway, we played the game and they got beat. We won! And what do you think? They cancelled the banquet and they took us to a field maintenance shed and put a hose in a knothole, I remember, and they said "You guys take a shower with this." That was it. So we said "Well, we're going to go back to L.A. to the Miyako Hotel where we're staying and they have a Japanese tub, so we'll take our shower there. That's how they took their ball games... seriously! (Jack Fujino, 8/22/1996)

Not all of the games were so serious. Moon Ikeda and his wife Chiyo remembered the Asahi playing "donkey baseball" at Washington Park in Santa Clara. In donkey baseball, all the fielders except the pitcher and the catcher were required to ride donkeys. A batter would bat normally, but if he got a hit, he had to ride a donkey around the base paths. Chiyo remembered George Yoshioka had trouble staying on the donkey. Moon recalled a batter getting a hit to the outfield and the outfielder beating him to first base with the ball because his own donkey would not budge!

When the team was playing at their home field, it became a regular practice for the players to change into their uniforms at Minato's Bath House on Sixth Street. After the game, they would go back to Minato's, bathe, and then change back into their street clothes. They would then go across the street to the Ken Ying Low restaurant:

After the games, the Issei who'd organized the team, they had a place on Sixth Street called Ken Ying Low, they'd already organized for us after the game. We'd take a bath in that *furo* house [bath house] on Sixth Street, then go eat China *meshi* [food] and go home. (Jack Fujino, 8/22/1996)

There was no specific organization that backed the Asahi; it was just a group of individuals. Mr. [Fudetaro] Horio used to give us each fifty cents after a ball game. Heck, we'd go to Ken Ying Low, have dinner, and we'd have change. It cost us like twenty-five or thirty cents a piece.

We'd go to a place like Stockton to play. I remember going there and eating lunch in a Japanese restaurant for like twenty cents. Of course, we had to pay for our own there, but they always had a bath house where we changed our clothes. Those were really good days. Those big bathtubs were made out of concrete and the sides were a little bit rough so you could scratch your back on there, it was so good. Minato's had one there, two houses away from the corner of Sixth and Jackson. That's where we used to dress for our San Jose home games. (Frank Shimada, 11/22/1996)

With many road games each year, travel was a part of the experience in the Japanese leagues. For many of the players, it was a very important part. Jack Fujino talked about the road trips:

We'd all jump in each others cars and we'd leave that morning if it was close, like Stockton, Alameda, and those places. If we'd go to L.A. or San Pedro, we'd have to leave early one day to play the next. It was about a three-day trip at least. That was a long trip for us in those days.

The Grower's Supply softball team played in the eight-team Washington League and except for the sponsor Phil Cuffaro, who played first base, the team was made up entirely of San Jose Asahi players. Phil Cuffaro owned the Grower's Supply, which occupied the old Okida store premises. This August 8, 1935, photo shows off the team's new uniforms. Back row, from left, George Ichishita, Harry Yoshioka, Phil Matsumura, unidentified man, Phil Cuffaro, George Yoshioka, "Moon" Ikeda; Front row, Chick Hinaga, Adrian Onitsuka, Joe Jio, "Blackie" Ichishita, George Hinaga, Yo Kanemoto. Collection of the Ikeda family.

To all of us ball players, we enjoyed that. You can challenge other teams; go to this city and that city. I think it was quite important to all of us. We didn't have any other areas to extend ourselves into, the baseball was about it. That gave us ball players an extra chance of meeting different town people. (Jack Fujino, 8/22/1996)

For 1937, league play was off again. Jim Uyemura with the *Nichi Bei Shimbun* wrote about the upcoming season:

This year, it appears unlikely there will be any class A circuit in Northern California....However, independent games will be played in San Jose under the co-management of Phil Cuffaro and Chicky Hinaga, and out-of-town teams desiring games with the Asahis should communicate with either Cuffaro or Hinaga at the Growers Supply, 201 Jackson Street. (*Nichi Bei Shimbun,* 4/17/1937)

George Hinaga was one of many very talented Asahi players. George caught the eye of a scout in 1936 and wound up playing professionally for the Vancouver Asahi in 1937. George is shown here in his Vancouver uniform. Collection of Pat Adachi.

Fresh out of high school, George Hinaga was making an impression with his sensational fielding and timely hitting. Playing with both the Asahi and the semi-pro McElroy Cheim teams in 1936, George caught the eye of a scout and was given a tryout with the Oakland Oaks. Recommended to the Vancouver Asahi, George played for the team in 1937. This was good timing, as it was a quiet year for San Jose without the NCJBL competition.

With the reorganization of the Northern California Japanese Baseball League for 1938, the old rivalries flared up for an exciting season. The teams included San Jose, the Lodi Templars, the Alameda Taiiku-Kai, the Stockton Yamatos, and the Sacramento Mikados. San Jose and Lodi battled it out for first place throughout the season, with the usually strong Stockton Yamatos struggling to stay out of the cellar. A new man in the Asahi line up was another Kanemoto brother, Masaji, helping out at first base. George Yamaoka joined the team as a catcher, with Jack Fujino playing in the outfield. Also, Sheik Uyejo appeared briefly as an outfielder.

George Yamaoka was known as a bright player and a natural leader, respectfully nicknamed "The General." George often caught for Asahi pitching ace Henry "Lefty" Honda:

> George Yamaoka used to give me hell all the time. George was a good catcher; he says "I want you to keep that ball inside, not outside!" I'd say "George, I'm trying like hell, but I can't keep it inside." You know, you get the feeling where you might hit somebody if you keep throwing all the time inside. I know when you're a left hander throwing to a right hander, it's hard to hit that inside pitch. George was sharp, always on top of the game. (Henry Honda, 5/21/1998)

League play was suspended over the July 4th weekend, when San Jose played a three-game series against the visiting Fresno Taiikus, Central California champions. Fresno won the first game 13–10. San Jose won the second and third games 11–6 and 15–14.

The Asahi Juniors were still solid competition, though it appears that they received occasional help from the regular team members to fill in gaps. Asahi Juniors team members for this year included Clark Taketa, Mori Shimada, Henry Honda, Jim Nagahara, Jim Kasano, "Moose" Hayano, Ed Kanemoto, Bobby Onitsuka, Frank Sakanishi, Ed Yoshioka, H. Ito, Watanabe, Esaki, and Iso Sasao. Most of these players would move up to the regular team within the next two years. The team was still being coached by Nobe Yoneda, but now listed Clark Taketa as manager.

The Asahis' regular season ended with the Templars' defeat of the Yamatos, giving them the right to meet the Asahi in a three-game series for the NCJBL championship. The Asahi won the series in early August. What had become clear though was that the Asahi and the Yamatos now had a very tough competitor in the Templars, who had developed an airtight defense built around their infield crew of Tom Ishida, Johnny Hiramoto, Matsuo Okazaki, and Kiki Hiramoto. Both the Asahi and the Templars had ended the season with a 7–1 record.

On August 28, 1938, the *Nichi Bei Shimbun* made its "All-Star Nine" selection. The first team selection included George Hinaga at third base, Harry Yoshioka in center field, and Harry Kanemoto, pitcher.

Another member of that years' all-star team, Stockton's second baseman Kenso Nushida, was the Pacific Coast League's first Japanese American player. He debuted for the Sacramento Senators on August 10, 1932, against the Missions. At 5′ 1″, 109 pounds, he did not have a 90-mph fastball, but he had great control, often confusing batters by throwing sidearm or occasionally using a submarine delivery. He pitched eleven games for the Senators with two wins and five losses.

Another occasional opponent for the Asahi was the San Luis Obispo Young Men's Buddhist Association. Jack Fujino told of a humorous incident during one of those visits:

The San Jose Asahi prepare to face their traditional rivals, the Fresno Taiikus on July 3 and 4, 1938. Fresno won the first game, but San Jose went on to win the second and third to win the series for this year. Asahi players from left are Frank "Blackie" Ichishita, George Yoshioka, Jack Fujino, Frank Shimada, George Yamaoka, Sheik Uyejo, Adrian Onitsuka, Masaji Kanemoto, Chick Hinaga, Harry Kanemoto, Harry Yoshioka, Yo Kanemoto, George Hinaga, Russell Hinaga. Two players to the right of Russell is Fresno's legendary Kenichi Zenimura. Collection of the author.

We played in San Luis Obispo and they had a pretty good team. In those days, sometimes when you go to visit, you don't know where you're going to play. A lot of those teams don't have a home diamond like we did. Outside of their playing field there was a tomato patch.

This guy got up and hit a long fly ball over the left fielder's head and he chased after it and then went to pick up the ball. He picked up the first one he came upon. The ball was dirty, but he threw it in anyway. (Jack Fujino, 8/22/1996)

Joe Jio also recalled the incident:

We threw it to third and got the guy tagged out. When they threw the ball in to the pitcher, Russell, he's cagey, so when he saw it was a practice ball, he held it for a while then threw it into our dugout and they threw out a new ball. (Joe Jio, 8/18/1996)

There are slightly different versions of this story; one has Russell throwing one pitch to make the wrong ball "official" before discarding it. Also, some think Joe Jio was the fielder who found the ball, another thought it was Harry Kanemoto, and another who was sure it was Harry Yoshioka. Joe Jio later recalled that the player they tagged out was Carl Taku.

At thirty years old, Joe Jio was a reliable veteran who had been with the team over ten years. Frank Shimada remembers joining the regular team and being surprised at the age of some of the players:

I remember Joe Jio when he played left field for us; he was our lead-off man. I used to think "Gee, what an old guy!" He was almost ten years older than I was. They said he had a good eye and a wide stance like Joe DiMaggio. (Frank Shimada, 11/22/1996)

The year 1939 was a big year for rookie players on the Asahi. Joining the regular team that year were Henry Honda, Bobby Onitsuka, Jim Nagahara, Moose Hayano, Carl and Roy Shimizu, Mori Shimada, and Ed Yoshioka. Yo Kanemoto and Adrian Onitsuka had left the team and Chick Hinaga appears to have been on a one-year hiatus. Jack Fujino also left but would return for the 1941 season. Besides having a team of excellent hitters, the Asahi also had a number of talented pitchers; in 1939, Henry Honda was the latest addition to the pitching staff:

During the summer [of 1938] I started playing for the Asahi "B" team. In 1939, I played for the Asahi "A" team. I got a lot of experience in high school and when I got to the Asahi I was fortunate that there were some good baseball players. Pitchers like Blackie Ichishita, he used to be a pitcher before he hurt his shoulder. He helped me my first time when I went out there. How to get on the mound, how to wind-up, throw, throw with runners on base, pick-off move, and things like that.

I did real well the first year, but I did better the following years, 1940 and 1941. I guess 1940 and 1941 were the two best years I had with the Asahi. (Henry Honda, 5/21/1998)

Blackie Ichishita had been playing first base for many years, his height giving him a good reach for throws that might not be perfectly thrown. His brother George had also pitched for a while. Currently the team had pitchers in Harry Kanemoto, George Hinaga, Frank Shimada, Henry Honda, and of course, Russell Hinaga. Harry was known for a fast, sidearm pitch, George for a stealthy hook, Frank for sweeping curves, Henry for his fastball and sliders, and Russell for his sharp breaking curves and tricky change of pace.

Besides managing the team, Russell was spending quite a bit of time on the other side of the plate as a catcher. Moon Ikeda's wife, Chiyo, recalled that Russ was known as "Mr. Baseball." Over the years, Russ would fill in where needed, often playing in the outfield or not playing at all. Most of the players shared this selfless attitude, playing where and when they were needed. With the Asahi doing so well in pitching, it was not often that Russ got called upon anymore. When the situation required it though, Russ was more than willing to go out and give it all he had, as Henry Honda remembered:

In 1939, we went to play down south. We played against the San Fernando Aces the first game, then the next day we had a game with the Skippers in San Pedro. I pitched the Saturday game against San Fernando. I went nine innings and I was sick that day, car sick. I still pitched and we lost.

The next day we went to play the Skippers and Harry Kanemoto was supposed to pitch. Somebody threw him a ball and he went to catch it with his bare hand and split his hand between the fingers. They had to take him to the doctor and get it sewn up. So he was done, he couldn't pitch any more.

Russell Hinaga, who hadn't pitched in a couple of years, said "I'll go pitch." He went out there and pitched the whole game and we beat the Skippers! That was amazing! You know how hard it is to pitch a ball game when you're not in shape? (Henry Honda, 9/19/1996)

Russell's daughter Lillian remembered going to the games when her dad played, "I remember going, but I never watched him play, I was so busy going up and down [the grandstand steps]. It was an outing for us."

With their strong pitching staff and heavy hitters like George Yoshioka, George Hinaga, newcomers Bobby Onitsuka and Frank and Mori Shimada, the Asahi had yet another successful season. Also, it did not hurt that their pitchers were all good with the bat. Once again, they were to face the intimidating Lodi Templars. Unlike the previous season, however, the Asahi were unable to prevail, and the Lodi Templars won their first NCJBL championship.

While the members of the Asahi baseball team all had their own unique abilities, one thing that they all shared was a love of baseball. This love revealed itself in dedication to the team and hard work. They were aware that playing well was not only satisfying to themselves, but to their fans as well:

> We used to practice twice a week with the Asahi. Wednesday and Friday, something like that, but twice a week. Most every Sunday we had a ball game, usually at 1:00 p.m. The farmers had to work, but they came. They'd get up early in the morning and go to work, get the produce packed and everything, then head over to the game. That's what we had to do too, we had to help. (Henry Honda, 9/19/1996)

The NCJBL expanded from five to eight teams between 1939 and 1940, even with the loss of Sacramento. The league now consisted of the Sebastopol Sakuras, the Lodi Templars, the Walnut Grove Deltans, the Oakland Merritts, the San Jose Asahi, the Mt. Eden Cardinals, the Alameda Taiiku-Kai, and the Stockton Yamatos.

These new teams provided the league with a lot of talent and keen competition. Four games into the 1940 season, new field manager George Yoshioka found his Asahi in the middle of a four-way tie for second place. Sebastopol was in first and the strong Alameda and Stockton teams were in the cellar. By the end of the season, San Jose and Lodi were once again on top. In another three-game series, San Jose won the first game 5–2. Phil Matsumura wrote in the August 23, 1940, *Nichi Bei Shimbun:*

> Last Sunday's Asahi triumph over Lodi in the first game of a playoff series for the N.C. loop title is still being verbally played in San Jose as the rabid fans re-enact the game play-by-play and comment endlessly on the various features of the tussle. Orchids are unsparingly directed to veteran chucker Russell Hinaga for this brilliant twirling that silenced the heavy-hitting Tokay boys for six innings. Likewise the fans are loud in their praise for the great relief work of George Hinaga, who after taking over the mound duties with the bases loaded, set the next ten batters down in easy manner.

Unfortunately for the Asahi, the Templars took the next two games, winning the championship for the second year in a row. The final game featured the successful pitching combination of Russell and George Hinaga in a very tight 3–2 contest. Kaz Ito threw a great game for the Templars, fending off the Asahi attack. "Shot" Iwamura in left field and George Takeuchi at shortstop both turned numerous potential hits into sensational outs.

Pitcher "Red" Tanaka, third baseman Matsuo Okazaki, and left fielder "Shot" Iwamura were the Lodi selections for the first team of the NCJBL All-Star team. Russell and George Hinaga were selected for the Asahi as catcher and shortstop, respectively.

The Asahi's Final Inning

The following year the NCJBL season opened on May 4. Although no one realized it at the time, 1941 would be the Asahi's final season in San Jose. George Yoshioka and Masaji Kanemoto were lost this year to the draft. Joe Jio, Harry Yoshioka, Frank Ichishita, and Harry Kanemoto had retired. Frank Sakanishi also left, intending to return at a later date. Jack Fujino had returned, however, and the Asahi still presented a formidable team.

Jack Fujino took over at first base, Mori Shimada was at second, Bobby Onitsuka played third, George Hinaga was the shortstop, and Jim Nagahara, Ed Yoshioka, Mits Kobayashi, and George Sakamoto were in the outfield. George Yamaoka did most of the catching, while Henry Honda and George and Russell Hinaga handled most of the pitching. Henry also played right field and Russ also played third base.

Stockton was making an effort to return to the glory it had once known. By mid season, the top three positions were held by Lodi, Stockton, and San Jose, respectively. Although Walnut Grove had withdrawn from the league, competition was keen as usual. For example, in a game between Lodi and Alameda, first baseman Tom "Mushy" Ishida pulled the old hidden ball trick on base runner Min Ota. In a completely legal maneuver, the baseman conceals the ball, pretending that it has been returned to the pitcher. If the runner begins his lead off the base before realizing the situation, he can easily be tagged out by the baseman standing near him.

From mid season, the Asahi began their ascent to the top of the standings. In one game against the Stockton Yamatos, Stockton had built up a 5–2 lead into the last half of the seventh inning. At that point, Tom Okagaki and Frank Shimada both got to base on errors and then scored on Bobby Onitsuka's hit. Russell Hinaga came up to bat and hit a home run to bring home Onitsuka. The Asahi brought the score to 6–5. They then made two more runs in the bottom of the eighth, making it 8–5. In the final inning, Henry Honda struck out the remaining batters to win the game.

In a very tight battle between San Jose, Stockton, and Lodi, the title series came down to San Jose and Stockton. In the first game, played at Graham Field in San Jose, Stockton won 15–4. Stockton was on the crest of a winning streak; the five-hit pitching of Shim Shimasaki and Stockton's strong hitting made them a formidable opponent. Vowing to end the series with a win in the second game, Stockton lost to the Asahi 14–6 at the Yamato Grounds in Stockton. Strong Asahi hitting and poor fielding by the Yamatos gave San Jose the win. The third and deciding game of the series was played on Sunday, September 14, 1941, back at Graham Field in San Jose. San Jose trailed by a single run into the eighth inning, when the Yamato bats came alive. George Hinaga got nailed for three more runs in the eighth. Henry Honda came in for the ninth inning but to no avail. The Yamatos continued their onslaught and won by the final score of 10–2.

Despite their third championship series loss in a row, the boys from San Jose displayed their typical good sportsmanship. Following the game, San Jose hosted a banquet for the Yamatos at Ken Ying Low. Afterwards, the two teams participated in an all-star bowling meet at the Palace Alleys on Santa Clara Street.

This was not to be the Asahi's final bow, however. The Asahi had agreed to play in a benefit game with the Permanente Cement nine later that evening. The Permanente team was the state amateur champion. Jack Fujino remembered the game well:

> One time there was a team in San Jose called the Permanente Cement Company. They formed a team of all the local "hot-shots," good ballplayers. What happened was that they won the state title and came home and wanted to play the Asahi to make money to go to Michigan to play for a national title. We were supposed to be cinches.

San Jose Asahi Reunion. In the summer of 1994, Joe Jio hosted a reunion with many of his old teammates in San Jose's Japantown. This was the author's first opportunity to meet most of the players, and it was quite a thrill to sit with them listening to the stories and the banter. Clockwise from left, Frank Shiraki, Adrian (Onitsuka) Yamamoto, Yo Kanemoto, Harry Yoshioka, Dr. Tokio Ishikawa, Joe Jio, George "Moon" Ikeda, George Hinaga, Chick Hinaga, Frank Shimada, Jack (Ota) Fujino. Collection of the author.

They asked us if we would play them and make some money, so we went to Washington ballpark and played. Russ Hinaga pitched, I caught, and what do you think? They lost the ballgame, we beat them! They were so mad; they cancelled the trip to Michigan.

I remember that game especially. Every time we'd come in to bat, we'd run to third and first base to coach the players on the bases. You'd have to pass in front of the Permanente dugout and gee, you ought to see the names they called us. They were mad and they just took it out on us. They were nice fellas, but some of them were really mean. (Jack Fujino, 8/22/1996)

Jack Fujino later recalled anecdotally that his car keys had come out of his pocket while sliding into second base and that the game came to a brief standstill while he searched for them. Phil Matsumura described the game in an article for the *Nichi Bei Shimbun*:

Completely baffling his hard-hitting and dangerous foes, Russell Hinaga hurled one of his greatest games to hand the state amateur champion Permanente Cement nine, a 6–4 lacing at Washington diamond in Santa Clara last Sunday night. The net proceeds of $65 were contributed toward a fund to send the Cementers to Battle Creek, Michigan for the national American Baseball Congress. Latest report disclosed inability of the team to make the trip due to lack of sufficient funds.

The triumph was beyond the wildest dreams of the Asahis' supporters. To come back after the afternoon's loss of the deciding game in the NCJBL play-off series to Stockton, was a fitting climax to a successful season and a tribute to veteran Hinaga's years of top-notch performance for the San Jose team.

With a dexterity that comes only with years of experience, Hinaga mixed his sharp breaking curves with tantalizing slow balls so well that the first nine Cementers to face him went out in consecutive order. It was not until the fourth inning that Tamone, lead-off man, connected for the first hit off Hinaga.

Permanente committed five costly errors, but it was the skillful base maneuvers and heads-up performance that enabled the Nisei nine to outscore the classy amateur titlists. The Asahis tallied one in the first, second and third and added two more in the fifth plus another in the sixth to complete its scoring while the opponents were held to one run in the fourth, fifth and two in the last inning.

Permanente threatened dangerously in the final inning putting two men on after two had scored. With its clean-up hitter Cantell at bat, Hinaga was in a tight spot but held him to a weak single to fill the bases. Anello was forced to ground out to Shimada to end as thrilling and spine-tingling a game as the Asahi fans would want and gave the local Nisei team its prize victory of the year. (*Nichi Bei Shimbun,* 9/17/1941)

The NCJBL first team all-star selection for 1941 included pitcher Henry Honda, catcher Russell Hinaga, and third baseman George Hinaga. The third team selections included Asahi Ed Yoshioka in right field. That year, for the first time, an "All-NC" rookie team was selected. The rookie selection included Asahis Tom Okagaki at shortstop and Frank Shimada in right field.

The San Jose Asahi had been the "Headquarters" club for the 1941 season. As such, they hosted a dance at Tracy Gardens outside the city limits on Stevens Creek Road. George Yamaoka, Jack Fujino, and Clark Taketa were responsible for the event that was intended to become an annual event. Music was provided by the "rhythmic jives" of the Al Davina Orchestra.

During intermission, a championship trophy was presented to the 1941 champions, the Stockton Yamatos. Receiving the league's cup for the best hitter was Mike Kawaoka, the unheralded slugger from the Sebastopol Sakuras. The leading pitcher honor went to Henry Honda. The most valuable player award went to Russell Hinaga. The choice was based on all-around capabilities, sportsmanship, and inspirational qualities. The award, which could not have come at a better time, was a fitting tribute to a man who had given so much to his community and his team.

A Veteran Retires

Russell Hinaga's wife, Mitsuye Hinaga, was born in the United States but spent most of her childhood in Japan. She returned to the United States in 1922 when she was 14. Mitsuye fondly recalled how Russ first got her attention: "I went to see the movie, Japanese movie, you know, Okida Hall. He is staying upstairs. He throw to me one time, two time, he throw to me peanuts! He must like me!" (Mitsuye Hinaga 11/19/1996). Although Mitsuye did not go to baseball games or really understand them, she knew what she was in for when marrying Russell: "He's a good pitcher, that's all I know. I have to understand that he has to go all over the place to pitch." (Mitsuye Hinaga, 11/19/1996). Their daughter Helen said that

Pictured on the left is Russell Hinaga's NCJBL Most Valuable Player award for the 1941 season, his last with the San Jose Asahi. On the right is a clock given in appreciation of Russell's long career, inscribed: "To R. H. From The Asahi Club 1918 to 1941." Collection of the Hinaga family.

her father and uncles had established a name for themselves: "As we were growing up, everywhere we went and said our last name, they'd say, 'Are you Russell's daughter?' The name was so connected with baseball. With three brothers on the same team, they made such a reputation." (Helen Hinaga Imagawa, 11/19/1996).

Although Russell's playing days in the Japanese leagues ended with the 1941 season, his involvement with Nisei baseball would continue for many more years. His daughter Helen reflected:

> My dad had four daughters. To carry on his baseball, there was no one. He kept saying "I like girls anyway." And my Uncle George had four daughters. So my dad tried to teach the first grandson that came along, Mark. I remember he was outside in the backyard and he was saying "Okay, you hold the ball like this." I had heard how good he was with this certain way he threw the ball; I mean he could really strike out a lot of people. So I was thinking to myself, "Gee look, he was just trying to teach Mark how to throw the ball!"

> Dad enjoyed sports so much and especially baseball and he was able to relate to the very young and the very old alike. I heard from one of his friends, that one thing my father did was to help all the Issei that came, because they couldn't speak the language.

> He'd be the central figure in Japantown. Everybody would say "Oh, here comes Russell!" When he passed away at 72 [in 1975], they all said that he'd lived a very full and happy life (Helen Hinaga Imagawa, 11/19/1996).

Chapter 6

BASEBALL UNDER THE GUARD TOWERS

"When we went to
Santa Anita,
my brother Mori said,
'Let's form our own team.'
So we got all the
young guys out of the
old Asahi team like
Tom Okagaki, Chi Akizuki,
Tom Kawahara, Carl Shimuzu,
and Tom Sakamoto
to coach us and
we made our own team."

Frank Shimada

Japan's attack on Pearl Harbor on December 7, 1941, affected the lives of all Americans, particularly those of Japanese descent. General John L. De Witt, Commander of the Western Defense Command, was empowered by President Roosevelt to declare "military areas" and exclude "any and all persons" from them. On March 2, 1942, General De Witt declared California and parts of Oregon, Washington, and Arizona to be strategic areas and those persons of Japanese ancestry would be removed from them. The Japanese community had little time to prepare for their departure. The fortunate ones were able to make arrangements with non-Japanese friends or acquaintances to watch over their property. These arrangements were usually satisfactory, though not always.

Asahi Field had been an issue for some time because of the expense of maintenance and the availability of other fields. Henry Honda recalled the condition of the field towards the end:

> It used to be a pretty good ballpark. Since 1939 or 1940, George Hinaga and I used to go over there with our trucks and mow the lawns. It was nothing but hay out there, like a hay field, not good to play ball on. We used to drag the field and put the bases in and fix the pitcher's mound. Right about before the war time, they were trying to talk Tommy [Sakamoto] and Harry [Hashimoto] into signing the papers so they could sell it. Tommy and Harry wouldn't sign. We didn't play there anymore in 1941, it was so run down. The field, the bathroom was bad, so nobody used it and nobody wanted to put any money into it. Most of the time we played at Washington Park, Graham Field, and Backesto Park. (Henry Honda, 9/19/1996)

In those final years, the field was sometimes made available for other uses. Sumito and Ralph Horio remembered a destruction derby and a motorcycle race, neither of which improved field conditions. In the fall of 1941, Asahi Field was also known as San Jose Motordrome, with a 1.5-mile oval track in the field. Harry Hashimoto, Tom Sakamoto, and Russell Hinaga did not want to give up the community's ball field, but the war with Japan sealed the park's fate. Asahi Field was sold in early 1942 prior to the evacuation of Japanese nationals and Japanese Americans from the West Coast.

To the Assembly Center

On May 24 and 25, 1942, Japanese living in Santa Clara County registered with the Wartime Civil Control Administration control station in the men's gym at San Jose State College. From May 26 to 29, special trains began running to transport the Japanese from San Jose to the Santa Anita racetrack near Los Angeles. This would be their home for the next five months, before moving to a relocation camp being constructed at Heart Mountain, Wyoming.

No sooner did the Japanese begin arriving at the Santa Anita Assembly Center than they began to become organized. Camp life became a microcosm of their lives on the outside and there was something for everyone to do. The Japanese love of sports flourished in camp and soon an assembly center newsletter began covering camp sports news:

> Santa Anita's hardball season opens with a practice game between Three Star and San Pedro Saturday at the Anita Chiquita field.
>
> The game begins at 1:30 and is to be played on the new diamond on the south-west corner of the field.
>
> On Sunday the San Jose B's face the Commandos in the morning game, and the San Jose A's take on the All Stars in the afternoon.
>
> So far seven teams have signed up to play and other teams and players are invited to sign up at the Recreation department. They must have their own equipment. (*Santa Anita Pacemaker,* 6/16/1942)

Besides baseball, popular sports activities also included softball, basketball, football, volleyball, golf, sumo, and judo. With only a few exceptions, like the Asahi, the dozens of sports teams that organized at Santa Anita had predominately English names. Some of the more interesting names included the Stablemates, the Nine Old Men, and the Jr. Nips. The San Jose Asahi had more than enough players (including players returning from retirement) to field a team, so some of the younger Asahi decided to create their own team. Frank Shimada and his brother Mori were instrumental in its formation:

> In 1941, we were getting some of the younger guys coming in out of high school into the Asahi team. It looked like a lot of them weren't getting much of a chance to play; the old timers were playing more or less. When we went to Santa Anita, my brother Mori said "Let's form our own team." So we got all the young guys out of the old Asahi team like Tom Okagaki, Chi Akizuki, Tom Kawahara, Carl Shimizu, and Tom Sakamoto to coach us and we made our own team. (Frank Shimada, 11/22/1996)

Frank went on to explain how they decided on a name for the team:

> We were all working on camouflage nets for the military and we all got together outside and sat around by a big

> fountain they have over there. We wondered "What should we call ourselves?" Then somebody, I can't remember who it was, suggested we name ourselves Azucars. That was the horse that won the first Santa Anita Handicap. (Frank Shimada, 11/22/1996)

League play began on Saturday, July 18, 1942, with seven teams in the "A" league: the Asahi, the Azucars, the Dodgers, the Oldsters, the Padres, San Pedro, and the Three Stars. The first game was between the Dodgers and the Anita Oldsters at the Anita Chiquita diamond. Ceremonies were held prior to the game honoring Los Angeles Nippons baseball star Pete Kondo, who had been disabled four years earlier in an automobile accident. Many of the players that day were former teammates of Pete's. Pitching for the Oldsters was George Matsuura, a Los Angeles Nippon pitcher who had played briefly in 1936 for the professional Nagoya baseball team in Japan. The Dodgers defeated the Oldsters 18–8.

The following day, the San Jose Asahi played San Pedro and the Azucars played Three Star. The Asahi won their game 18–1, and the Azucars won their game 10–2.

One highly anticipated game was played on August 8, between the Azucars and the Asahi. The camp newsletter ran the following article on the upcoming game:

> The colorful San Jose Asahis will try to stop the Azucars, A hardball co-leaders, in the feature game at England field, 2 p.m., Saturday.
>
> Undaunted by their 6–7 defeat by the Dodgers last week, the veteran Asahis are gunning for a victory over their former teammates to stay in the running for the championship.
>
> The Azucars must hurdle the Asahis to keep in stride with the Dodgers.
>
> Mainstays of the speedy Azucar outfit are Tom Okagaki, shortstop, and Mori Shimada, second baseman, both leading hitters on last year's Asahi teams, Lefty Kitahara, Chitoshi Akizuki and Frank Shimada.
>
> San Jose's well-balanced nine includes George Yamaoka, Russ, Chickie and George Hinaga, Joe Jio, Roy Shimizu and Frank Shiraki.
>
> Tom Sakamoto is the Azucar manager and Clark Taketa is manager of the San Jose Asahis. (*Santa Anita Pacemaker,* 8/5/1942)

The Azucars won the contest and went on to defeat the Dodgers for the Center hardball championship: "In Santa Anita we beat everybody, including the old Asahi guys! There must have been thousands of people out there to watch the younger guys play the old timers." (Frank Shimada, 11/22/1996).

Heart Mountain Relocation Center

Japanese from various assembly centers began arriving at Heart Mountain Relocation Center as early as mid-August 1942. The camp newsletter, the *Heart Mountain Sentinel*, started up soon after internees began arriving from Santa Anita. An article in the first issue of October 31, 1942, focused on the arriving San Jose athletes: "San Jose dominates the sports brigade. The Zebras, a powerful basketball aggregation of San Jose boys, are here en masse....The Azucars, baseball champions at Santa Anita, and the San Jose Asahis are among the others receiving laurels at the assembly center." Singled out for mention were Chitoshi "T-Bone" Akizuki, a Zebra basketball player and Azucar center fielder; Tom Okagaki, batting king of the Azucar team; George Hinaga, who played on both the Asahi baseball and the Zebra basketball teams; and pitcher Frank Shimada of the Azucars.

The softball season was starting at that time and Frank Shimada was the chairman of the softball leagues. The leagues included six teams in the senior or "A" league and four teams in the "B" league. One of the "B" league teams was the newly formed San Jose Zebras softball team, taking its name from the San Jose Zebras basketball team. They would eventually become an "A" league team. Chi Akizuki recalled:

> At Heart Mountain the first thing we did was have like a social club, a Zebra Club. We had dances, parties, then the basketball team and the baseball team. The majority of the Azucars became Zebras. The older people were really interested in watching the baseball. They could follow baseball better than basketball. (Chitoshi Akizuki, 12/13/1996)

Two Zebra ballplayers, Chitoshi Akizuki and Tom "Chesty" Okagaki, had fathers who had been strong Asahi supporters. Chitoshi's father was Masuo Akizuki, who had helped the first Nisei team get its start back in 1918. Tom Okagaki's father, Kichitaro, had served as manager for the Asahi's trip to Japan in 1925.

Hardball games got underway at Heart Mountain on Sunday, June 6, 1943. Play began with several weeks of exhibition games, allowing the development of the following teams: the Bears, the Huskies, the Northerners, the Sportsmen, the Taihei, and the Zebras. With many members of the old San Jose Asahi joining the break-away Azucars, the two teams were essentially reunited. Following the lead of the Zebras softball team, the Asahi and Azucars were reborn as the San Jose Zebras baseball team.

An article in the *Heart Mountain Sentinel* ran just prior to the opening game between the Zebras and the Huskies on June 6, 1943, describing the recently completed baseball diamond in block 26: "The local diamond has no fence with the right field boundary out some 450 feet from home plate while the left field road is approximately 350 feet away." (*Heart Mountain Sentinel,* 6/5/1943).

The Huskies defeated the Zebras 15–10 in a game that featured the pitching of not only Frank Shimada, but also of Russ Hinaga and Adrian Onitsuka. An estimated 2,500 fans turned out for this opening game. "Grey-Haired" Russ Hinaga supplied the surprise of the day with a triple over left fielder Chi Omori.

The camp newsletter reported on an exhibition match between the Asahi and the Zebras:

> The Zebras meet the Asahis at 2 p.m. today in a "young men vs. oldsters" affair.…This afternoon's "civil war" contest will find Shimada opposing Hinaga and Jack Tono. Shiraki, Jio and Ichishita are big stickers for the Asahi team which is manned by old-time greats, some of whom will never see 40 again. (*Heart Mountain Sentinel,* 6/12/1943).

The Asahi and Zebras were locked in a close 7–6 struggle in the sixth inning when the game was called on account of a thunderstorm. Although the Asahi were no longer playing official games, they played occasional nostalgic exhibition games, a tradition that would continue into the 1950s.

On June 26, 1943, the hardball season began with the six aforementioned teams, though the Bears had changed their name to the Shinkos and the Taiheis eventually changed their name to the Mustangs.

The current roster for the Zebras was Jack Tono, Russ Hinaga, George Yamaoka, Rosie Matsui, George Yamamoto, George Hinaga, Tom Okagaki, Joe Jio, Chi Akizuki, and Tom Kawahara.

With four wins under their belt, *Heart Mountain Sentinel* sportswriter Mits Inouye proclaimed that the Zebras had "all but sewed up the Heart Mountain Baseball pennant." (*Heart Mountain Sentinel* 7/31/1943).

On July 31, the Zebras played the title game against the Huskies at 2 p.m. on the block 26 diamond. The score remained tied for the first three innings, but in the fourth, the Zebras made eight runs on seven hits, two walks, and three errors. They continued to score in the fifth, sixth, seventh, and eighth innings, winning the game 18–7. Jack Tono pitched for the Zebras, holding the Huskies to one run in the innings he pitched. The Huskies made a valiant effort in the ninth against reliever Russ Hinaga, when they picked up six additional runs. Joe Jio provided four runs in the seventh inning when he hit a grand slam. Chi Akizuki won the batting crown for the season with 11 hits in 19 at bats for a .579 average.

Mits Inouye ran a biographical sketch of Russ Hinaga's 25-year career in his July 31 news column. He wrote that Russ had over 200 wins to his credit, and in one game in Japan, Russ caught seven men off base. Mits also mentioned that Russ had at one point been offered a contract by the Tokyo Giants. He concluded by saying that Russ considered Kenichi Zenimura of Fresno his greatest rival on the diamond.

Following their championship win, the Zebras played a series of two games with the all-stars of the other teams. In the first game, Jack Tono started for the Zebras and was relieved by Russ Hinaga to save the game. The Zebras won 13–12. In the second game, George Hinaga took to the mound for an exciting ten-inning game. "Rosie" Matsui's home run in the tenth provided the winning margin. The Zebras won that game 6–5.

During this time, Heart Mountain also received occasional visits from teams in nearby towns for exhibition hardball or softball games.

League play began again on August 14, 1943, this time with four teams competing in the "A" league; the Zebras, the Huskies, the Sportsmen, and the Northerners.

After winning their first game, the Zebras dropped out of the league. The Zebras had received an invitation from Kenichi Zenimura at the Gila River Relocation Center in Arizona to participate in a baseball tournament. With George Yamaoka helping with arrangements, the Zebras accepted the invitation. Adrian Yamamoto, who had recently changed his name from Onitsuka, was one of the players who made the journey:

> In the war time, we went to play in the Arizona camp from Heart Mountain, Wyoming. They had a team from every block, I think. We played for two weeks against different teams. Zenimura's the one who got us over there. He paid our fare. They collected admission to see the games and they made enough that they gave us eating money too. They treated us good over there, they fed us everyday. We played everyday except we used to rest on Monday. We had a lot of fun. It was during war time so, you're not supposed to travel, but they let us go. It was pretty good! (Adrian Yamamoto, 10/27/1996)

Sportswriter Jack Kunitomi described the tournament:

> Winning 8 out of 13 games in 14 days was the enviable record set by the San Jose Zebras in their games with Gila teams. The record is all the more remarkable when the roster of the Zebras included only 13 players, of whom only three were regular pitchers.
>
> Unaccustomed to the torrid heat of the desert which reached as high as 120 degrees after supper when most games were played, the San Jose lads tired easily. Several players also suffered from some sort of an injury during

the series. Rosie Matsui, Chi Akizuki, Chesty Okagaki and Carl Shimizu were bothered by bone bruises and split fingers.

...[George Hinaga] was scheduled to pitch five games, but worked in only two games. He was given credit for both games, although brother Russ came to his rescue during one game. The elder Hinaga surprised everyone by working in seven games, five of which he won. He proved to be the workhorse of the series by pitching 21 innings in three consecutive days. His ability to work in those games was partially explained by the hot weather which loosened his aged right arm. Lean Jack Tono did not fare so well as the others, working in four games and receiving credit for one win.

The best game in the series was with the Guadalupe nine, winner of the first half of the Gila baseball league, the Zebras losing by a heart-breaking 3–2 score. This game drew 5,000 fans and was played in the incredibly short time of one hour and twenty minutes. Practically all the games were completed in an hour and forty minutes which shows the high caliber of the teams in Gila. Pitching and batting of the teams there proved a definite obstacle for the locals and most of the players were surprised that they won the series.

...The players were unanimous in their approval of the sportsmanship and hospitality shown by the Gilans. Treated like royal guests, the Zebras had nothing but praise for their hosts. (*Heart Mountain Sentinel,* 9/18/1943)

With the Zebras dropping out of league play in the second season, the Sportsmen became the second half champions. A championship was held between the winners of the first and second seasons on September 25. With Jack Tono pitching, the Zebras took the crown by a score of 8–2.

The Heart Mountain "A" league hardball season for 1944 began on May 13, with six teams once again competing: the Zebra Ayes, the Zebra Bees, Block 20, Block 27, the Sportsmen, and the Amateurs. Mixing things up a bit and providing more balanced, competitive teams, several Zebras left the main team to beef up the "B" team, Block 20, and the Amateurs. Russell Hinaga moved to the Zebra Bees with his old Asahi battery mate Frank Shiraki. Tom Okagaki and Tom Kawahara joined the newly formed Amateurs. Another old Asahi, Blackie Ichishita, joined Rosie Matsui on the Block 20 team. Helping the versatile George Hinaga on the Zebra Ayes with pitching chores was Billy Shundo. The only other Zebras to remain from the previous year were George Yamaoka, Mori Shimada, and Chi Aki-zuki. Mori was hurt early on with a bone chip. When the Zebra Ayes played the Bees, it was referred to as a "family squabble."

The Zebra Ayes, hurt by the loss of George Hinaga and George Miyahara to active military duty, did not take first place this season; however, Russ Hinaga and the Zebra Bees did. Because of a disagreement with the decision of an arbitration board regarding a game, the Zebra Bees dissolved in protest. They reemerged the next season as the Oldtimers.

The second season got underway on Saturday, July 1, with the Zebra Ayes victory over Block 20, 11–10. The Zebra teams united on July 4 for an exhibition game against an all-star team comprised of the best players from the other teams. Russ Hinaga pitched, allowing eight scattered hits and striking out nine batters on the way to an 8–4 win over the All-Stars.

The Zebra Ayes took the title for the second season. Beating the strong Oldtimers in an 8–7 game that went 10 innings, they then took the title game against the Amateurs. The 1944 championship series would now be played by the first half champion Zebra Bees (now Oldtimers) and the second half champion Zebra Ayes. The Ayes won the first game 9–6, and the second game on August 20, 9–4 to capture the crown. Billy Shundo, the ace pitcher for the Zebra Ayes, also won the batting crown with a .480 average, getting 12 hits in 25 attempts. Oldtimer Russ Hinaga rated with a respectable .333, hitting 11 in 33 at bats.

The 1944 Heart Mountain hardball champion Zebra Ayes. Back row, from left, Keiichi Ikeda, Bob Sugita, Billy Shundo, Tak Sugiyama, Tasku Yamada; Front row, George Shiraki, Chi Akizuki, Norman Yasui, Mori Shimada, Fumio Kusunoki. Collection of Chitoshi Akizuki.

The Gila All-Stars then arrived for a series of games in September. Originally intended to be an 11-game series, 13 games were played from September 2 through September 17:

> When we were at Heart Mountain, the Zenimura boys came to play against the Heart Mountain team. Here they came and played and I was like twelve. I saw the Zenimura brothers and they must have been about sixteen or seventeen. I wanted to meet them, so my dad [Russ] got me to go to where all of the players were and I got their autographs.
> (Helen Hinaga Imagawa, 11/19/1996)

With the strong pitching of Tak Abo and George Fujioka, the Gila All-Stars swept the first six games against the Zebra Ayes and Bees, the Amateurs, and Block 20. Veteran Kenichi Zenimura worked behind the plate and also pitched in the series.

On September 9, the first of a five-game series between the Gila and Heart Mountain All-Star teams began. Although missing George Hinaga and Tasku Yamada, George Iseri pitched Heart Mountain to its first win over Gila (5–4). George also won the second game 3–2. In the third game, George Fujioka gave Gila its first win, 15–9, over Heart Mountain.

The fourth and deciding game of the all-star series featured Russ Hinaga as the starting pitcher. Limiting Gila to four hits, Heart Mountain won the game in a 6–0 shutout. Though Heart Mountain had taken the all-star series three games to one, the fifth game was played anyway, with Gila winning to give them two for five in the series.

Gila won nine out of the thirteen games played during their visit, winning their last game in an 8–0 shutout of the All San Jose team. The *Heart*

Speedy Chi Akizuki gets a hit in one of the All-Star games held at Heart Mountain in 1944. Collection of Chitoshi Akizuki.

The Heart Mountain Zebras won their third consecutive championship in 1945. Back row, from left, Mori Shimada, Chi Akizuki, Ernie Inouye, Fumio Kusunoki, Shig Tachibana, Tabo Shimizu, Tom Okagaki; Front row, Tak Sugiyama, Keiichi Ikeda, Shozo Hata, Russell Hinaga, Hachiro Shimada. Collection of Chitoshi Akizuki.

Mountain Sentinel sports staff elected Kenshi "Harvey" Zenimura and Tak Abo as the most outstanding Gila players and Mori Shimada the most outstanding for Heart Mountain. Harvey Zenimura, 15, was also the youngest member of the Gila team. Harvey went on to play professional ball on the Japanese Hiroshima Carp from 1952 through 1955. Harvey's brother Kenso "Howard" also played on the team for a while in 1953. Both Kenishi and Kenso were the sons of Kenichi Zenimura.

The 1945 season opened with games on April 7, 1945. The teams for that year included the Zebras (no "Bees" this year), the Amateurs, the Sportsmen, the Block 20 "Elites," and two new teams; the Maryknolls and the Heart Mountain Juniors. The Maryknolls included the talented Billy Shundo, Babe Nomura, and veteran Frank Shiraki. The Heart Mountain Juniors were made up entirely of the previous year's "B" team players.

Playing for the Zebras this year were Chi Akizuki, Keiichi Ikeda, Tak Sugiyama, Mori Shimada, Fumio Kusunoki, Shig Tachibana, Shozo Hata, Russ Hinaga, Tabo Shimizu, Hachiro Shimada, Tom Okagaki, and Ernie Inouye. An "A" league rookie that year, Ernie Inouye would pitch two one-hit games this season and set a Heart Mountain strikeout record of 16 batters, passing the previous mark of 12 held by Amateurs pitcher George Iseri.

After the end of the first half, the Sportmen, continually hampered by relocation, withdrew from the league. They were soon replaced by the Oldtimers.

The championship game was played between the Zebras and the Amateurs on July 16. The batteries were George Iseri and Fuzzy Shimada for the Amateurs, and Ernie Inouye and Mori Shimada for the Zebras:

> Behind Ernie Inouye's masterful five-hit twirling, the Zebras toppled the Amateurs, 5–1, in a twilight game here Monday before 2,000 fans to annex the local class A baseball championship for the third straight year....(*Heart Mountain Sentinel,* July 21, 1945)

This brief article appeared in the final issue of the *Heart Mountain Sentinel* on July 28, 1945:

> The Zebra baseball team, champions for the third consecutive year, held a championship dinner recently at 24–27. General arrangements for the chicken dinner were made by Coach Mori Shimada, who returned last week to San Jose with three teammates, Hachiro Shimada, Shig Tachibana and Buddy Takata.

於鶴嶺湖朝日野球團記念寫眞
千九百四十五年

The 1945 Tule Lake Asahi. Back row, from left, unknown player, Hugo Nishimoto, Oscar Itani, George Nakano, Ralph Horio, Frank Horio, Yoshio Takayama, unknown player, John Horio; Front row, Hiro Morimoto, unknown player, George Nakao, Sumito Horio, Ted Sakamoto, remaining unknown. Collection of Ralph Horio.

Among those who attended the affair were Tak Sugiyama, Keiichi Ikeda, Bob Sugita, Fumio Kusunoki, Ernie Inouye, Russ Hinaga, and Bert Shimane. Special guests were Tosh Asano, Kaz Shimizu, Min Yoshizaki and Roy Yamadera. (*Heart Mountain Sentinel,* July 28, 1945)

Asahi at Other Relocation Camps

While the San Jose Asahi name was essentially retired with the move from Santa Anita Assembly Center to Heart Mountain in 1942, an Asahi offshoot still existed in 1945 in Tule Lake Segregation Center. Nearly half the team consisted of the San Jose Horio clan, who had moved to Placer County hoping to avoid being sent to a relocation center but were eventually sent to Tule Lake anyway. While in Placer County, Sumito, Ralph, John, and Frank Horio formed the Hillmen baseball team that took the Tule Lake hardball championship in 1943. Jiggs Yamada's brother Mike was also a member of the team.

Henry Honda wound up in the relocation center near Topaz, Utah, where softball was the preferred game, to Henry's chagrin: "I couldn't play baseball, so I was running the softball league. It held me back because I couldn't play for almost three years before I went in the army. I finally started playing in the army and I got back into shape again. Especially being a pitcher, you've got to keep your arm in shape all the time." (Henry Honda, 5/21/1998).

Baseball, and sports in general, was clearly instrumental in normalizing camp life, not just at Heart Mountain, but at each of the ten relocation centers located throughout the United States. It not only provided a healthy outlet and exercise for the participants, but gave everyone, young and old, something to look forward to.

With the end of the war and the closing of the camps, Japanese Americans reclaimed their lives as citizens of the United States. The road that lay ahead was not an easy one; many had to start from scratch, but it was a road that held the promise of a brighter future.

Baseball had played an important role in the pre-war communities of Japanese Americans. While baseball still played its part, its importance would gradually diminish and it would not enjoy the popularity it had once known. The barriers created by discrimination had begun to erode, sources of entertainment seemed to multiply, and baseball had other sports to compete with as the interests of younger generations expanded.

The Asahi name remains linked to that period of time before the world was shaken by war. By the war's end, the older Asahi had all retired and many of the younger Asahi had become Zebras. The torch had once again been passed, though this time not only to a new generation but into a new era.

Chapter 7

RISE
OF THE
SAN JOSE
ZEBRAS

"We didn't have anyone
else to pitch, so we
called Clark Taketa.
Clark says, 'Jiro Nakamura
will be on the plane,
pick him up in Salt Lake City'.
So he flew him to Salt Lake
City, we picked him up, he
pitched the whole game,
we won, and we flew him
back home!"

Henry Honda

Many of the young men at Heart Mountain had found their way into the army and did not begin returning to civilian life until 1946. It was then that Mori and Frank Shimada, who had formed the Azucars and Zebras in camp, began the task of rebuilding the Zebras as members returned to the Santa Clara Valley:

> I got back from the army in January of 1946 and we started the Zebra team that summer. Mostly my brother and I ran the whole thing, especially my brother Mori. He had all the equipment from Heart Mountain. Later on I did all the managing and set up the games and lined up opponents. Because there were no Japanese teams, I used to contact this guy in San Francisco, a sports shop over there used to line up games for all the semi-pro teams. That's how we played one year until some of the other areas got teams. (Frank Shimada, 11/22/1996)

The Zebra team at this time consisted of Ernie Inouye, Harry Ikebe, Babe Nomura, Frank, Mori, and "Fuzzy" Shimada, Sumito, Ralph, John, and Frank Horio, Henry Honda, Tom Okagaki, Shig Tachibana, Min Ando, Tom Ezaki, Chi Akizuki, Jim Nagahara, and Tom Taketa.

The San Jose Zebras in 1946 at San Jose's new Municipal Stadium. Mori and Frank Shimada began rebuilding the Zebras baseball team during the summer of 1946 with the assistance of Sam Della Maggiore as coach. Back row, from left, George Yoshihara, John Horio, Shig Tachibana, Frank Horio, "Fuzzy" Shimada, Coach Sam Della Maggiore; Middle row, Ralph Horio, Tom Okagaki, Frank Shimada, Harry Ikebe, Babe Nomura, Ernie Inouye, George Hinaga; Front row, Sumito Horio, Russell Hinaga, Henry Honda, Chi Akizuki, Mori Shimada, Jim Nagahara. Collection of the Honda family.

One of the Zebra's earliest games was played on June 23, 1946, winning against the Latin-American Cards at Graham Field. With John Horio pitching, the Zebras beat Fresno in an exciting 16–15 game on the Fourth of July at San Jose's new Municipal Stadium. Babe Nomura hit a towering 375-foot home run and Frank Horio hit four for six. In early August the Zebras had a seven-game winning streak before losing a close game to the semi-pro San Jose A's.

Henry Honda and George Hinaga both returned from the army in July and joined the Zebras soon after. The Zebras were now playing under the auspices of the Young Buddhist Association (YBA), which helped with equipment and other costs like the rental of the lighted Washington Park in Santa Clara for night game practice.

On August 18, 1946, the first of several post-war exhibition games was played between the Zebras and the "Oldtimers" Asahi baseball team. Joining Russell Hinaga on the Oldtimers were Frank Shiraki, George Yamaoka, Frank Ichishita, Yo Kanemoto, Jackson Kumagai, Ed Yoshioka, Harry Yoshioka, Joe Jio, and Lulu Yoshida. The Zebra "reserves" played this game, which ended in an 8–8 tie called in the seventh inning. Russ can be seen in many of the Zebra photographs from the mid to late 1940s, though not as a player. According to Henry Honda, Russ would often umpire and was otherwise considered the number one fan. He also coached a team called the San Jose Asahi Cardinals for a while.

The Zebras traveled south to Los Angeles for a Labor Day series against the Los Angeles Nisei All-Stars at Griffith Park. In the first game, the Zebras tied the game at 3–3 in the eighth inning, then on Babe Nomura's booming triple in the eleventh, the Zebras won 6–3. The second game was won by the All-Stars 7–4. Frank Shimada admitted to being involved in a minor incident during one of the games: "We played an all-star team down in L.A. right after the war and they had a black umpire there named Ashford or something like that. He became a major leaguer. I was arguing a call he made and I happened to bump him with my chest and he threw me out." (Frank Shimada, 11/22/1996).

Though the YBA Zebras were not in a league, their "season" was unquestionably successful, and a dance was held to celebrate it:

> The championship San Jose Zebra baseball squad will be honored with a post season dance this Saturday night from 8 o'clock at the local YBA hall.

> Completing one of the most successful baseball seasons in local annals, the Zebras were virtually undisputed leaders of Nisei nines in the state. Although they split even in the Southland with the L.A. All-Stars, the latter team was roundly trounced by the Monterey Presidio All-Stars last month.

The GI outfit was in turn twice defeated by the Zebras.

The local nine compiled a record 11 wins out of 13 contests against Nisei competition and took three out of five in semi-pro games. It scored at least one win over every major Nisei nine in the state, including among their victims Fresno, L.A., Placer County, Lodi, Suisun, Madrone and Watsonville Vets.

Credit for the success of the Zebras should go to Coach Sam Della Maggiore, who shaped a shaky and green outfit into a hustling and powerful aggregation. Mori Shimada organized the team and was manager for the season. (*Nichi Bei Times*, 10/4/1946)

The 1947 San Jose Zebras sporting new uniforms provided by the Young Buddhists Association. Back row, from left, Sumito Horio, George Hinaga, Fuzzy Shimada, Frank Horio, Tom Okagaki, Tak Abo, George Hashimoto, Jay Kakuchi. Front row, Chi Akizuki, Teruo "Ted" Sakamoto, Ernie Inouye, John Horio, Jim Yagi, Frank Shimada. Collection of Frank Shimada.

The Zebras were without Mori Shimada, Babe Nomura, and Henry Honda for 1947 but they gained the pitching and batting services of their old Gila River rival, Tak Abo. Also joining the Zebras for 1947 were George Hashimoto, Teruo "Ted" Sakamoto, and Jim Yagi. This year the Zebras donned their first team uniforms, compliments of the YBA. They also had the use of San Jose's new Municipal Stadium for most of their home games:

At Municipal Stadium, we were one of the regular teams out there. When it was first built there was hardly anybody playing in there. It was a beautiful ball park, all the other teams liked to come in to play us.

At Asahi Field, nobody hit it over the fence. We didn't have that kind of power. But at Municipal Stadium, for the first time some of our guys started to hit some over the fence. We had younger guys, maybe they were a bit stronger, maybe the bats were a little bit livelier. Babe Nomura, when he played for us, hit it over the center field fence at Municipal Stadium. My brother hit a couple over the fence in left field. George Hinaga did it. Art Kitahara never did hit one over that fence, but he did over in North Sacramento ball park. Right field was short, but they had that fence way up high and he clobbered it right over that fence. We had some strong hitters in the post war. (Frank Shimada, 11/22/1996)

Russell Hinaga and his old teammate Frank Ichishita survey the Zebras' activities at Municipal Stadium. Collection of Frank Shimada.

Many new teams came together in 1947 to form the Northern California Nisei Baseball League (NCNBL), with Clark Taketa as the league chairman. Besides the Zebras, participants included Sebastopol, Mountain View, San Francisco, Oakland, and Richmond. The East Bay Richmond team proved to be the Zebra's strongest competition and featured the sensational pitching and hitting of Jiro Nakamura, as well as Henry Honda and his talented brothers, Tom and Jim.

Playing a split season schedule, the Zebras won both the first and second halves to become the 1947 champions. Their final game was against the rival, Richmond Athletic Club. The Zebras held off a spectacular five-run rally in the ninth inning to win by a score of 9–8.

An awards dance was held at the Hotel DeAnza in San Jose. At that time, the Zebras were presented with the *Nichi Bei Times* permanent trophy and one-year custody of the Dr. Kimura perpetual trophy. The Most Valuable Player trophy went to Chi Akizuki. The leading pitcher was John Horio, who went undefeated in ten games.

For 1948, the NCNBL was divided into the Coast and Valley leagues. The Zebras played in the Coast league which included Richmond, Sebastopol, Mountain View, San Francisco, Oakland, Watsonville, and a new San Jose team, the Asahi Cardinals.

San Jose Asahi Cardinals

Roy Murotsune, who played on the Asahi Cardinals through 1950, told how the team got started:

> The one who started it was Naoaki Otomori. He said "Let's make a team and let the kids from San Jose play some baseball." So I went with him to see Carl Shimizu. Carl said "Hey, you let me play, let's make a team. I've got a few more hits left!" Then we went to see George Yamaoka. We used the Asahi uniforms and we formed a team. I don't know if George played or not, but he helped us.
>
> They had an "A" league and an "AA" league. We weren't good enough, so we played "A." In those days the recreation department, all we'd have to do is go over there and they'd set up a ball park for us. They had a small ball park at Backesto and a few times we played at Municipal. Most of the games we played at Backesto. One time we played at Washington Park in Santa Clara. Russ, he coached us one year. The way we played, he used to laugh at us! We had fun though. (Roy Murotsune, 8/9/2004)

Ed Yoshioka, Adrian Yamamoto, and the Horios also played on the Asahi Cardinals for a while. They eventually discarded their old Asahi uniforms for new Cardinals uniforms. Playing through the 1951 season, they continued to appear in news articles as the Asahi Cardinals, though often simply as the San Jose Cards. Other Asahi Cardinal players included Art Tanabe, Hank Nose, Asa Yonemura, Willie Yoshimoto, Mo Ohara, Vaughn Miyazaki, Hachiro Shimada, Harry Kawayoshi, and "Satch" Koyano.

Satch Koyano, who had been at Tule Lake Segregation Center with the Horios, was a talented pitcher. Clark Taketa had tried to get him to play for the Zebras, but Satch wanted to play with his friends, so he joined the Asahi Cardinals in about 1950. Satch did join the Zebras later after the demise of the Cardinals.

The Zebras, sporting their new pinstriped uniforms, had another winning year in 1948 and played against the Richmond Athletic Club for the Coast NCNBL title on August 15 at San Jose Municipal Stadium. George Hinaga led the hitting parade with two triples, two doubles, and a single in five at bats. Art Kitahara went three for four and Chi Akizuki got two important hits in a 20–5 rout over Richmond. Howard Zenimura helped the Zebras out at second base, while Zebras' founder Mori Shimada caught for the losing team.

The Zebras then went on to play a two-game championship series against the Valley League champion Florin Athletic Club, which at that time fea-

The San Jose Zebras huddle in this photo taken at Santa Clara's Washington Park in about 1949.
Collection of Frank Shimada.

tured the strong combinations of the four Tsukamoto brothers and the two Tahara brothers. The Zebras won both games, 8–2 and 6–1. Jits Hayashi and Mas Kinoshita pitched for the Zebras in the second game, limiting Florin to three hits. George Hinaga, Art Kitahara, Jits Hayashi, and Chi Akizuki led the Zebras attack, with George and Art each collecting homers.

In 1949, the NCNBL AA league was made up of the Fresno Nisei, Richmond Athletic Club, Suisun Athletic Club, the Walnut Grove Deltans, and the San Jose Zebras. As in the pre-war days, Fresno was a formidable rival. Mori Shimada had returned to the Zebras and joining the team were Frank Yoshioka and Jiro Nakamura.

It was about this time that Jerry Hinaga had come up from Los Angeles to visit relatives with his dad, Chick. Chick had moved his family to Los Angeles after the war so that his wife could be near her relatives. Jerry recalled that he was about 13 years old when his dad took him out to see his Uncle George and the Zebras play. As Jerry was sitting against a fence watching the game, the bat boy, dressed in his own Zebras uniform, got benched for some infraction of bat boy etiquette. The manager needed a replacement and he looked around:

> He looked at me and asked if I want to be a bat boy and I said yeah. Then he told me what to do as far as getting the bat out of the way when someone gets a hit. I remember he handed me a whole box of brand new baseballs and said to rub them down. So I got some dirt or something and rubbed them down. The name Jiro Nakamura just stuck with me, I was impressed with him. He was lanky, very tall. I remember being in the dugout, like being under the stands [probably Municipal Stadium]. These guys were cussing a lot and spitting chewing tobacco. (Jerry Hinaga, 6/3/2004)

San Jose had another good year in 1949 and faced Fresno in the title series. Fresno won the first game 3–1 in San Jose. The second game was played at Fresno State College field. John Horio and Mas Kinoshita did the pitching for San Jose, while George "Lefty" Fujioka of the Gila All-Stars pitched for Fresno. Among Fresno's talent were Harvey and Howard Zenimura and a recent acquisition, Fibber Hirayama. Like Harvey and Howard, Fibber would also go on to play with the Hiroshima Carp in Japan. Fibber had quite a career with the Carp, playing from 1955 through 1964.

Chi Akizuki opened the game with a single to left, stealing second, going to third on a catcher's overthrow, and scoring on Fujioka's wild pitch. San Jose scored again in the third on Tom Okagaki's grounder. It was not until the fifth inning that Fresno finally touched John Horio to tie the game up. Fresno put three more up in the sixth, sending Horio to the showers. Mas Kinoshita did not fare much better and Fresno continued to rack up the runs. The Zebras came back in the eighth to fill the bases with no outs. George Hinaga scored a runner on a single and Art Kitahara two more on a double. In the ninth, Sumito Horio and Tom Okagaki got on with two outs, but George Hinaga ended it on a popup to Fujioka. Fresno won with the final score of 9–5 to win the title series.

The following month, the Zebras took on the strong San Fernando Aces in a Labor Day series at Municipal Stadium. The Zebras won the two-game series, beating the Southern California champions twice, 10–7 and 13–5. Asahi alumni George Yamaoka caught the first game for John Horio. The battery for the second game was Mas Kinoshita and Fuzzy Shimada.

There was no "AA" league for 1950; however, the Zebras arranged to play independent games through August. Two exciting games were played with San Jose's traditional rival, Fresno. Fresno took the first game on June 18, with Fibber Hirayama pitching against Jiro Nakamura. Jiro pitched a good game, but Fresno bunched two hits, two walks, and an error for three runs in the third inning. Fibber shut out the visiting Zebras and Fresno won 4–0. In the second game played at Municipal Stadium on July 2, Fresno brought with them "guest" pitcher, Gordy Miyamoto from Monterey. San Jose nailed Gordy for five runs in the third inning, adding a few more to the tally later in the game. Jiro Nakamura pitched another great game for San Jose, this time holding Fresno to two runs. Sharp infield play between George Hinaga, Tom Okagaki, and Art Kitahara contributed greatly to the Zebras' 8–2 win. A third tie-breaking game was discussed later in the year, but did not materialize.

Fans take in a Zebras game at Municipal Stadium in the late 1940s. Collection of Chitoshi Akizuki.

Another game of note was an exhibition game between the Asahi Cardinals and the Asahi Oldtimers played on July 4, prior to a game between the Zebras and the Lodi Athletic Club. Scheduled to play for the Asahi Oldtimers were Joe Jio, Russell Hinaga, Tom Sakamoto, Clark Taketa, Frank Shimada, Johnny Kasano, Blackie Ichishita, Harry and Ed Yoshioka, Harry and Yo Kanemoto, Adrian Yamamoto, Moon Ikeda, George Yamaoka, and Frank Shiraki.

When the Asahi really got going back in the late 1910s, they played a lot of their games against non-Japanese teams. By 1950, this had become a rather common practice. While Japanese Americans have encountered discrimination in many forms throughout their history in the United States, there are few reports of discrimination occurring in the game of baseball. Frank Shimada recalled one time in the early 1950s that it did:

> This guy figured we were good enough to go play the Humboldt Crabs. Those guys were a top-notch semi-pro team up in that area. They wanted to put out publicity and wanted pictures of our guys, so we sent them some pictures up there. When they found out we were Japanese, they cancelled the game.
>
> That was probably the lowest point we ever had. We really wanted to go up and play those guys; we knew they had a good team. It was the only instance I can remember. It would have been great if we could have gone up there and beat them. (Frank Shimada, 11/22/1996)

In 1951, management of the Zebras was passed from Kiyo Nishiura to Shig Otani. Joining the team that year were "Duke" Murata and shortstop Sam Sugimoto. Towards the end of July, Shig announced that the Zebras were seeking games with other Nisei teams. Clark Taketa, president of the Sonen Kai and sponsor of the team, mentioned the possibility of the team traveling to Los Angeles for games. Clark is also occasionally listed as the team's business manager in *Nichi Bei Times* articles. In August, the Zebras defeated the visiting Utah All-Stars 12–5. John Horio pitched the game with a returning Henry Honda playing right field. The team had also picked up another pitcher this year, Junius Sakuma, who filled in other positions as well. Heavy hitter Joe Murakami also joined the team this year.

The Zebras split a two-game series with the visiting Los Angeles Nisei Trading over the Labor Day weekend. The Zebras again split wins with Fresno, beating them 13–7 in August and losing 7–4 in September.

For 1952 the Zebras continued playing independent games. They were joined this year by Tets Fujimoto and Koshiyama. The *Nichi Bei Times* reported that the leagues had been heavily affected by the draft for the Korean War.

Tak Abo and Henry Honda looking sharp in their pinstriped uniforms about 1952.
Collection of the Honda family.

The Zebras played a benefit game on May 21, 1952, against the highly vaunted Wieland Brewers. Pitching three innings for the Zebras was the venerable Russell Hinaga, who held the Brewers to two hits during his time on the mound. The Zebras won 8–5 and brought in $500.00 to benefit local little leagues. Two new players in the Zebra lineup were John Kimura and Hash Taketa.

The Los Angeles Nisei Trading swung into town again, this time for a three-game Fourth of July series. The Zebras won the first two games 6–5 and 8–3, before dropping a listless third game which was called at the end of the seventh inning by mutual agreement.

The Zebras in Utah

Soon after, the Zebras were invited by the Japanese American Athletic Union to play in their seventh annual baseball tournament. The tournament was being held in Ogden, Utah, July 25–27, 1952. The highlight of the season, Henry Honda remembered the tournament well: "When we got to Salt Lake City, they talked to the guy who ran the tournament and he said 'I didn't expect you guys here', so he had to make the schedule again. We said 'That's fine, we're here, we're gonna play!' It drew a lot of people too." (Henry Honda, 9/19/1996).

The Zebras' chances of winning the tournament were thought to be slim, especially when Jiro Nakamura cancelled out at the last minute. Relying on Henry Honda, John Horio, and Satch Koyano for pitching, the Zebras won their first game on Friday evening. When the Zebras won the semi-finals on Saturday, they realized that they had a chance to win the tournament:

> Mori Shimada was the manager. He started me and I went seven good innings, but the eighth inning came up and I couldn't get up off the bench, I was so tired. That's high altitude up there. I said "Hey Mori, you better get somebody out there to pitch for me, I can't make it." It was the first game I'd pitched that year. Satch Koyano relieved me and we won that game.

> The final game we had to play against Lodi, of all teams. I was surprised they were there and they were surprised we were there! They had this young kid, Tom Daijogo, he was a right hander, almost six feet tall. I knew his brother Jim pretty well. The kid just came up, he must have been twenty years old or something, and he was pitching some good games. We didn't have anyone else to pitch, so they called Clark Taketa. Clark calls us back and says, "Jiro Nakamura will be on the plane, pick him up in Salt Lake City." So he flew him to Salt Lake City, we picked him up, he pitched the whole game, we won, and we flew him back home! I think that was the first game he'd pitched all year. I don't know how he made it, because I ran out of gas. That high altitude really gets you. (Henry Honda, 9/19/1996)

With Nakamura pitching, San Jose beat Lodi 4–0 to win the tournament. Nakamura also won the "Most Valuable Player" award. Henry Honda and Chi Akizuki shared their thoughts on this highly regarded player:

> Jiro Nakamura played with us on Richmond A. C. He was a good pitcher; he was one of the best. I would say he was one of the best Nisei pitchers at the time, but he was too rowdy. He just didn't concentrate on the game. But boy, I tell you, he was a lot better than I ever was. He had a fast ball and a curve ball that dropped like Sandy Koufax, he was left-handed, too. (Henry Honda, 9/19/1996)

> We had this young guy named Jiro Nakamura. He was drafted by the Cincinnati Reds. He played with their farm team, the Modesto Reds. He was young and he didn't take care of himself. He was great, he was really great. In high school he used to win a lot of games 1–0, 2–0, 2–1.

In fact, one game when he was playing with us against a team of San Jose State players, he struck out eighteen of these guys and we beat them. He had a lot of talent. (Chitoshi Akizuki, 12/13/1996)

On June 21, 1953, the Zebras paid a visit to San Quentin penitentiary for a game against a prison team. Playing within the prison walls, the Zebras lost 8–7. Frank Shimada recalled that they faced a pitcher who had played for the St. Louis Browns.

Attendance to the games had been dropping to the point where, in August, the Zebras announced that they would only schedule more games if the fans would turn out.

New players on the Zebras this year included Allen Asakura in right field and Frank Murakami at second base. The team continued picking up games where they could, playing teams like Les Vogel Chevrolet, the Lucky Lager nine in Alameda, the Santa Cruz Seahawks, and the traveling Jeffersons, a well-known team out of San Francisco.

The invitational California Nisei Baseball Championship series began this year, with five teams competing at Lodi's Lawrence Park. The games were played from September 5 through September 7, between the San Jose Zebras, Lodi Athletic Club, Los Angeles Nisei Trading, the San Pedro Harbor Skippers, and the Sacramento Valley All-Stars.

The Sacramento Valley All-Stars won the tournament, beating Nisei Trading 9–5 in the final game. Lodi won the consolation finals over San Jose by the score of 6–2. Sacramento was presented with the 1953 tournament championship trophy and the *Nichi Bei Times* tournament perpetual trophy. To become permanent owner of the *Nichi Bei Times* trophy, a team had to win the tournament three times. All-Star selections for the tournament included San Jose's Art Kitahara (first base), Jim Honda (third base), Tom Okagaki (shortstop), and Chi Akizuki (outfield).

For 1954, the Zebras had scheduled a game against Waseda University who were planning a tour of the United States. Clark Taketa announced in late June that Waseda had to cancel the August 2 game due to passport problems. New to the team this year were Hideo Egawa, Chet Hamamoto, Toru Ito, Akira Itow, George Ochikubo, Tom Egusa, Sats Morimoto, Ben Kobata, and Jack Hayashi.

Besides independent games, the Zebras were playing in the Santa Clara Night Baseball league. On July 3 and 4, the Zebras played a holiday series with the visiting Little Tokyo Giants from Los Angeles. The Zebras took the first game 15–5 and the Giants took the second game 17–4. In a later series, San Jose and Lodi also split two games.

The second annual state Nisei baseball tournament was again held in Lodi over the Labor Day weekend. The Zebras won an opening round thriller from Nisei Trading. With the score tied 5–5 in the ninth inning, Joe Murakami hit a 350-foot home run to win the game. San Jose then went on to defeat the previous year's champions, the Sacramento Valley All-Stars, in the semi-finals. The Zebras finished second, however, losing the final game to the Placer JACL 7–1.

Joining the Zebras for the 1955 season were Jim Murakami, Ray Matsunaga, Earl Santo, Jim Ono, pitcher Shig Moriki, and Yas Ban at shortstop. The Labor Day tournament for this year was again played at Lodi. San Jose was eliminated in the first round and Placer went on to win the second year in a row by beating Lodi 21–15. Bill Nishimoto was voted MVP of the tournament.

The NCNBL reformed for 1956 with San Jose, Fresno, Lodi, Mayhew, and Walnut Grove competing for the championship. With new team member Kaz Hiramoto, San Jose won the first half going undefeated and Fresno won the second half also undefeated. The title match was played between San Jose and Fresno. The game was close until the bottom of the eighth inning when San Jose got six runs to insure their win. The final score was 11–4.

San Jose Zebras Reunion. In the spring of 2004, the author hosted a small reunion of Zebra players at his home in San Jose. They had the traditional Asahi lunch of "China meshi," watched home movies of Zebras games that Ralph Horio had filmed in 1948, and enjoyed going through Frank Shimada's photo album. From left, Ralph Horio, Adrian (Onitsuka) Yamamoto, Frank Shimada, Tom Okagaki, George Hinaga, Shig Otani, Chi Akizuki, Roy Matsuzaki. Collection of the author.

The Zebras did better in the 1956 tournament, making the finals for the first time since 1953. San Jose lost to Nisei Trading 10–3, with the L.A. pitching staff being credited for achieving their first title in the series.

In 1957, the Zebras welcomed new member Roy Matsuzaki to the team. Roy had played for Mayhew Athletic Club in Sacramento County since the early 1950s and became the player/manager soon after joining the Zebras:

> I was playing for San Jose City College. Shig Otani was the manager at the time and he was running the team. I was approached to play for the Zebras, so I joined them. I was asked why I don't take over as player/manager, which I did. I recruited high school players, just like Mr. Otani used to.
>
> I remember the Zebras were sponsored by the JACL, because I went to the meetings and they covered our insurance for us for a few years. As far as money and donations, the merchants here in Japantown supported us. (Roy Matsuzaki, 12/20/1996)

The 1957 NCNBL was made up of San Jose, Mayhew, Fresno, East Bay, Lodi, and San Francisco, with Fresno taking the championship.

This year the San Francisco Nisei brought home the *Nichi Bei Times* trophy for the first time. This was the same trophy that the *Nichi Bei Times* donated in 1953, and Manager Todd Kamiya returned it to the newspaper offices on Eddy Street. Repairs were made to the trophy which had lost all but the ankles of the figure mounted on the top.

By 1958, many of the original Zebras were gone. Frank and Mori Shimada, George Hinaga, Chi Akizuki, and Tom Okagaki had left. Ernie Inouye had pitched until his arm gave out. Two of the original players who did remain with the team through the final season were John and Frank Horio.

The team's new manager Roy Matsuzaki recruited many new players for this year, and they included Mike Matsuno, Stan Yasuda, George Yamasaki, Yosh Takaki, Kin Mune, John and Harry Shimizu, Vic Nakamoto, and Charlie Uchiyama. Roy had also brought Koji Watanabe and Bill Nishimoto to the team.

The NCNBL for 1958 was made up of the same teams with the exception of Lodi. Fresno once again took the championship, beating Mayhew 4–3.

The California Nisei Baseball championship for 1958 was won by the Los Angeles Nisei Trading nine in a fourteen-inning marathon against Fresno. The annual tournament was hosted by San Jose and played at the Municipal Stadium. Roy Matsuzaki recalled the annual event:

> In my day, we played in Labor Day tournaments. It was sort of an invitational tournament, one-game elimination. Certain teams could be selected. It's an invitational, so of course other teams from Fresno or Sacramento could say

"Hey, this team hasn't been picked, so let's get this guy and put him on our team." So they padded up the team. I recall playing for Fresno one year, because my team wasn't invited. You could do that. (Roy Matsuzaki, 12/20/1996)

San Jose Nisei Tigers

In 1959, Roy received a donation of used Tigers uniforms from Fred Silva, who had been Roy's coach at San Jose City College. Roy used them to replace the old Zebras uniforms and changed the name from San Jose Zebras to San Jose Nisei Tigers. This is reminiscent of the Zebras basketball team receiving used uniforms from San Jose State College in the early 1930s. The basketball team did not have a formal name at that point and were nicknamed Zebras by sportswriters for the wide stripes on the uniforms. Joining the Tigers for 1959 were Joe Futagaki, Hank Nose, Al Kogura, and Fred Igawa.

Lodi returned to the NCNBL this year with Mas Okahara managing. Fresno continued its domination of the league by winning both the first and second halves to become league champions for the third year in a row.

Under manager Sus Sato, Mayhew A. C. won the California Nisei Baseball championship for 1959, beating San Francisco 10–7 in the tenth inning of the championship game.

The San Jose Nisei Tigers improved in the NCNBL standings for 1960, tying with Mayhew for second place. New member Miles Yamamoto hit a homer in their final game against East Bay Athletic Club. Miles Yamamoto's father is Adrian Yamamoto who had been an Asahi as well as a Zebra at Heart Mountain. San Francisco was out of the league this year and Fresno once again claimed the championship. Other new members for the Tigers in 1960 were Chester Itow, Tad Narita, Gary Kanemoto, Frank Kurose, Min Ikeda, Joe Tenma, and Kaz Kitagawa. This year the Li'l Tokyo Giants won the state Nisei baseball crown for the first time, defeating the other Los Angeles team, Nisei Trading, 6–2.

The NCNBL for 1961 was composed of San Jose, Fresno, Lodi, and the East Bay. Fresno won the title giving them their fifth consecutive victory. The Fresno Nisei Merchants also took the Labor Day tournament this year with manager Hats Omachi, defeating the previous year's champion Mayhew A. C. 16–2.

Interest in baseball had been dwindling in San Jose's Japanese American community, with very few fans turning out for games, primarily just the families of the players. At the end of the 1961 season, the NCNBL disbanded, and the team decided to call it quits: "I guess we were too old and nobody wanted to play anymore. When we disbanded, the interest had dropped and a lot of the younger kids had decided that their interest in baseball wasn't there." (Roy Matsuzaki, 12/20/1996).

And so one warm summer day in 1961, the final inning was played, the final out was made. With little fanfare, the equipment was collected, players said their goodbyes, and parted company. This was a casual end to a team that had begun nearly fifty years before; the end of a team that had not only provided so much enjoyment for hardworking immigrants, but had brought generations, communities, and even countries together. So, while the Asahis and the Zebras had their share of defeats, their story is ultimately one of victory.

As the world changed, so did the Japanese American community. Opportunities now existed beyond the borders of the community and life had become somehow busier for everyone. Growing competition from other sports also played a role in the team's demise. The Zebras basketball team fared better and is still in existence.

While it was an end of a team and perhaps an era, it was not the end of baseball in San Jose's Japanese American community. Eventually the question was once again asked, "Hey, why don't we start a team?"

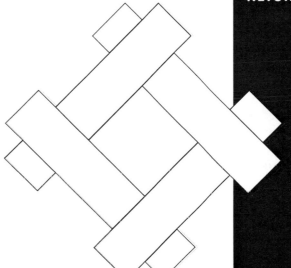

Chapter 8

San Jose Japanese Community Youth Service

The San Jose Japanese Community Youth Service (CYS) was organized in 1962 by several Japanese American organizations, including San Jose's Japanese American Citizen's League, the San Jose Buddhist Betsuin, and the local Veterans of Foreign Wars. The CYS was formed to provide healthy activities for children by a number of families under the leadership of Dr. Tom Taketa.

The CYS initially offered basketball, baseball, dance, band, and track, competing locally, in Southern California, and in Hawaii. Currently, the basketball, baseball, track, and dance programs still continue. A tennis program was added in 1974, a volleyball program in 1993, and a golf program in 1999.

Participants have gone on to play on high school junior varsity and varsity teams, college teams, and even professional teams. Many of the original participants have brought their own children into CYS activities.

A very early photo of the CYS baseball team taken in Los Angeles about 1963. Collection of John Yoshihara.

San Jose Youth Club

The San Jose Youth Club baseball team was organized in 1979 for Japanese American youth 14 and older by Shig Shimada. Shig was the younger brother of Mori and Frank Shimada and had been a bat-boy for the San Jose Zebras baseball team. Henry Honda's son Ron played for the team for many years and assisted with coaching and other responsibilities.

The San Jose Youth Club won the NCJBL Championships in 1983, 1985, 1989, and 1991. Other clubs in the NCJBL included the San Jose Royals and teams in Lodi, Florin, and San Francisco. The San Jose Youth Club won the California State AA Tournament Championships in 1989, 1993, 1994, and 1995. They also won the San Jose Invitational in 1982 and 1993. The team's final season was in 1995.

Shig Shimada, younger brother of Frank and Mori Shimada, started the San Jose Youth Club baseball team in 1979. Back row, from left, Coach Roy Murotsune, Danny Watari, Eric Yamasaki, Ron Honda, John Yoshihara, Dave Kawamoto Jr., Manager Shig Shimada; Middle row, Jay Jinguji, Randy Nishijima, Ken Yasuda, John Fukuda, David Yasuda; Front row, Gerald Ishimaru, Brian Iwashita, Larry Utsurogi, Mark Maruyama. Collection of Roy Murotsune.

San Jose Royals

In 1986, a number of players from the San Jose Youth Club decided to form a second team, the San Jose Royals. Founding members included Aaron Tachibana, George and Gerald Ishimaru, Dave Kawamoto Jr., Larry Utsurogi, Brian Iwashita, Ken and David Yasuda, as well as Coach Roy Murotsune. In 1988, Fred Watanabe, whose son Chris had joined the team, accepted the position of manager and remained through the team's final season in 1998. Fred's widow Carolyn tells about the years when Fred managed:

> I have many fond memories of all the fun times we had watching the Royals play ball. We developed statewide friendships as the team traveled throughout California in league competition every year and on our trips to L.A. for the California State AA Tournaments held down south every other year.
>
> The Royals players, parents, and relatives all contributed food for the banquets, and we had sponsors who financially supported us through donations towards ads for our program booklets during the tournaments which led to the funding for the next baseball season.

Fred would have loved to see the Royals continue to play baseball; however, it was getting more difficult finding players to play the entire season. The boys had other commitments, such as college, jobs, and family obligations that kept them from playing the entire season, especially when it was time for the tournaments at the end of the season.

The San Jose Royals won the NCJBL Championships in 1988, 1992, and 1997. They won the California State AA Baseball Tournament Championship in 1991 and the San Jose Invitational in 1986, 1987, 1988, and 1995.

The San Jose Royals in 1991 after winning the California State AA Baseball Championship title. Back row, from left, Coach Fred Kido, Lance Nakamitsu, Wes Tachibana, Aaron Tachibana, Kevin McCarsland, Todd Shimizu, Jim Wakayama, George Haruta, Reggie Higashi, Jeff King, Coach Rod Sekimoto; Front row, Manager Fred Watanabe, Ryan Fujikawa, Gerald Ishimaru, Steve Sekimoto, Brian Iwashita, Chris Watanabe, Jason Matsuoka, Darren Kurose and Coach Roy Murotsune. Collection of Roy Murotsune.

BOOKS

Adachi, Pat. *Asahi: A Legend in Baseball: A Legacy from the Japanese Canadian Baseball Team to its Heirs.* Etobicoke, Ontario: Coronex Printing and Publishing, 1992.

Barzun, Jacques. *God's Country and Mine: A Declaration of Love Spiced with a Few Harsh Words.* Boston: Little, Brown, 1954.

Johnson, Dan. "Japanese Baseball's Magical Moment." In *Jim Allen's 1996 Guide to Japanese Baseball,* edited by Jim Allen. Tokyo, Japan: Slug Books, 1996.

Klevens, Robert. *The Sports Card Heaven Guide to Japanese Baseball & Baseball Cards.* Davie, FL: Robert Klevens, 1991.

Lukes, Timothy J., and Gary Y. Okihiro. *Japanese Legacy.* Cupertino, CA: California History Center, 1985.

Miike, Fred N. *Baseball Mad Japan.* Tokyo, Japan: F. N. Miike, 1955.

Misawa, Steven, ed. *Beginnings: Japanese Americans in San Jose.* San Jose, CA: San Jose Japanese American Community Senior Service, 1981.

Nagata, Yoichi, and John Holway. "Japanese Baseball." In *Total Baseball,* third edition, edited by John Thorn and Peter Palmer. New York: HarperCollins, 1993.

Nakagawa, Kerry Yo. *Through a Diamond: 100 Years of Japanese American Baseball.* San Francisco: Rudi Publishing, 2001.

Niiya, Brian, ed. *More Than a Game: Sport in the Japanese American Community.* Los Angeles: Japanese American National Museum, 2000.

Obojski, Robert. *The Rise of Japanese Baseball Power.* Radnor, PA: Chilton Book Company, 1975.

Spalding, John E. *Always on Sunday: the California Baseball League 1886 to 1915.* Manhattan, KS: Ag Press, 1992.

Uhlan, Edward, and Dana L. Thomas. *Shoriki: Miracle Man of Japan: A Biography.* New York: Exposition Press, 1957.

JOURNALS AND MAGAZINES

Nagata, Yoichi. "The First All-Asian Pitching Duel in Organized Baseball: Japan vs. China in the PCL." *Baseball Research Journal* 21 (1992): 13–14.

Puff, Richard. "The Amazing Story of Victor Starffin." *The National Pastime* no. 12 (1992): 17–19.

Roden, Donald. "Baseball and the Quest for National Dignity in Meiji Japan." *The American Historical Review* 85 (June 1980): 511–534.

NEWSPAPER ARTICLES

San Jose Mercury Herald sportswriter Jack Graham began running a regular column on local baseball in 1922, and his were the first published accounts found of the San Jose Asahi baseball team's early years. Jack Graham died in May 1934.

Graham, Jack. "Japanese Asahi and Fourth Wards to Play," *San Jose Mercury Herald* , 5/7/1922.

Graham, Jack. "Japanese Teams Will Tangle This Afternoon," *San Jose Mercury Herald* , 5/2/1924.

Graham, Jack. "Local Japanese Trim Meiji Nine by Score of 6–3 in Snappy Game," *San Jose Mercury Herald* , 5/4/1924.

Graham, Jack. "Asahi Team Will Play Portland," *San Jose Mercury Herald*, 3/18/1925.

Graham, Jack. "Portland Beavers Trounce Japanese Asahi Club 8–1," *San Jose Mercury Herald*, 3/19/1925.

Graham, Jack. "Asahi Club Drops 6 to 4 Contest to San Jose Nine at Sodality Park," *San Jose Mercury Herald*, 8/31/1925.

Graham, Jack. "Asahi at Franklin," *San Jose Mercury Herald*, 3/25/1934.

"Jack Graham's Funeral Services Set Tomorrow," *San Jose Mercury Herald,* 5/30/1934.

"Funeral Services This Morning for John M. Graham," *San Jose Mercury Herald,* 5/31/1934.

"Play Local Japanese Team Today," *San Jose Mercury Herald*, 3/27/1935.

Kettman, August G. "Pitcher Hinaga's Single with Bags Loaded in Ninth Wins for San Jose," *San Jose Mercury Herald*, 3/28/1935.

When the San Jose Asahi toured Japan and Japanese-occupied Korea, the following article appeared in the Japanese language newspaper *Keijo Nichinichi* published in what is now Seoul, Korea.

"Peninsula Champion Defeated by Narrow Margin," translated by Yoichi Nagata. *Keijo Nichinichi,* 5/19/1925.

The *Nichi Bei Shimbun* (also known as *The Japanese American News*) was published between April 3, 1899, and May 3, 1942, in San Francisco. The first mention of the San Jose Asahi in this newspaper was in 1925. The newspaper resumed publication after World War II on May 23, 1946, and it changed its name to the *Nichi Bei Times*. The newspaper is still published today.

"San Jose Asahi Triumphs over Fresno," *Nichi Bei Shimbun*, 10/27/1925.

Koba, Fred. "Good Sportsmanship," *Nichi Bei Shimbun*, 1/1/1926.

"Stockton Yamatos Vanquish San Jose Asahi," *Nichi Bei Shimbun*, 7/6/1926.

"Asahi Apply for Membership in League," *Nichi Bei Shimbun*, 7/15/1926.

"S.J. Asahi Ball Team Gives Social, Dance Wednesday," *Nichi Bei Shimbun*, 11/30/1926.

"San Jose to Tackle Keio Tomorrow," *Nichi Bei Shimbun*, 6/13/1928.

"San Jose Asahis Swamp Pola Team 8 to 0 Last Sunday," *Nichi Bei Shimbun*, 7/17/1929.

"Formation of Bay Baseball League Is Held Likely," *Nichi Bei Shimbun*, 3/4/1930.

Uyemura, Jim. "No Northern California Class 'A' Baseball Loop This Season," *Nichi Bei Shimbun*, 4/17/1937.

Matsumura, Phil. "San Jose Asahi Meet Lodi Templars in Doubleheader This Sunday at Tokay Field," *Nichi Bei Shimbun*, 8/23/1940.

Matsumura, Phil. "Russell Hinaga Hurls San Jose to Brilliant Victory over State Champs," *Nichi Bei Shimbun*, 9/17/1941.

Suzuki, George. "Japanese Baseball Team 1st formed in U.S. 37 Years Ago," *Nichi Bei Shimbun*, 1/1/1941.

"San Jose Zebra Nine To Be Feted at Dance," *Nichi Bei Times* 10/4/1946.

San Jose residents of Japanese descent spent five months at the Santa Anita Assembly Center in 1942. Baseball activities at the center were reported in the *Santa Anita Pacemaker*, published between April 18 and October 7, 1942.

"Practice Opens for Hardball," *Santa Anita Pacemaker*, 6/16/1942.

"Asahis To Tackle Azucars Saturday," *Santa Anita Pacemaker*, 8/5/1942.

Most of the San Jose Asahi were interned at the Heart Mountain Relocation Center in Wyoming. Baseball activities at the camp were reported upon in the *Heart Mountain Sentinel*, which was published between October 24, 1942 and July 28, 1945.

"Good Santa Anita 'Material' Sent Here," *Heart Mountain Sentinel*, 10/31/1942.

"Baseball Opener Scheduled," *Heart Mountain Sentinel*, 6/5/1943.

"Improved Zebra Nine Meets Huskies Tomorrow," *Heart Mountain Sentinel*, 6/12/1943.

Inouye, Mits. "Sport Tidbits," *Heart Mountain Sentinel*, 7/31/1943.

Kunitomi, Jack. "Sport Tidbits," *Heart Mountain Sentinel* 9/18/1943.

Yamamoto, J. K. "He and Japantown Grew Up Together," *Hokubei Mainichi,* 1/1/1990.

INTERNET   "History." *San Jose Japanese Community Youth Service Handbook.* Rev. 2003. http://www.sanjosecys.org/CYSHandbook.pdf

INTERVIEWS

Chi Akizuki
interviewed 13 December 1996

Masashi Jack Fujino
interviewed 22 August 1996

Chickayoshi Hinaga
interviewed December 1996

George Hinaga
interviewed 23 August 1996

Jerry Hinaga
interviewed 3 June 2004

Lillian Hinaga
interviewed 19 November 1996

Mitsuye Hinaga
interviewed 19 November 1996

Henry Honda
*interviewed 19 September 1996
and 21 May 1998*

Ralph Horio
interviewed 7 March 2004

Sumito Horio
interviewed 15 August 1996

George and Chiyo Ikeda
interviewed 23 August 1996

Helen Imagawa
interviewed 19 November 1996

Dr. Tokio Ishikawa
interviewed 15 August 1996

Joe Jio
interviewed 18 August 1996

Grace Kogura
interviewed 17 June 2004

Roy Matsuzaki
interviewed 20 December 1996

Aiko Mune
interviewed 19 November 1996

Roy Murotsune
interviewed 9 August 2004

Tom Okagaki
interviewed 17 February 2004

Frank Shimada
interviewed 22 November 1996

Esau Shimizu
interviewed 27 September 2004

Frank Shiraki
interviewed 13 September 1996

Carolyn Watanabe
interviewed 31 December 2004

Harry S. Yamada
*interviewed 23 October 1993
and 13 September 1996*

Adrian Yamamoto
interviewed 27 October 1996

INDEX

116